RECONSTRUCTING DEI

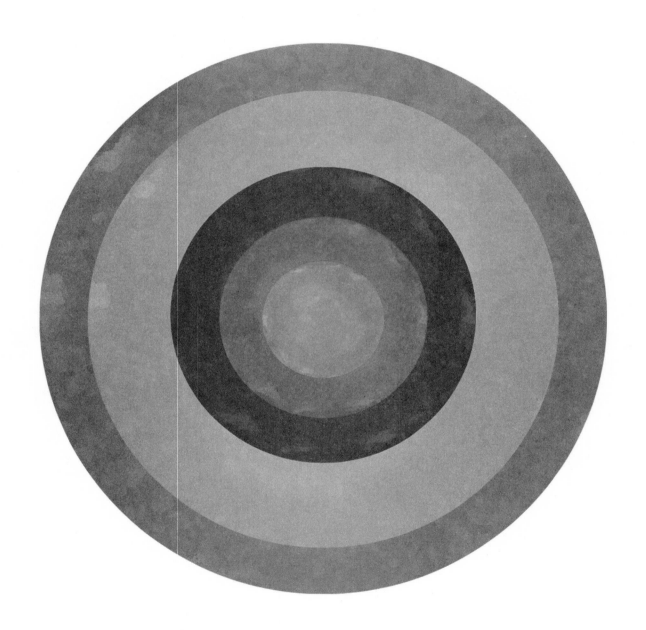

reconstructing
DEI

A PRACTITIONER'S WORKBOOK

LILY ZHENG

BK®
Berrett–Koehler Publishers, Inc.

Berrett-Koehler Publishers, Inc.
1333 Broadway, Suite 1000
Oakland, CA 94612-1921
Tel: (510) 817-2277
Fax: (510) 817-2278
www.bkconnection.com

ORDERING INFORMATION

Quantity sales. Special discounts are available on quantity purchases by corporations, associations, and others. For details, contact the "Special Sales Department" at the Berrett-Koehler address above.

Individual sales. Berrett-Koehler publications are available through most bookstores. They can also be ordered directly from Berrett-Koehler: Tel: (800) 929-2929; Fax: (802) 864-7626; www.bkconnection.com.

Orders for college textbook / course adoption use. Please contact Berrett-Koehler: Tel: (800) 929-2929; Fax: (802) 864-7626.

Distributed to the U.S. trade and internationally by Penguin Random House Publisher Services.

Berrett-Koehler and the BK logo are registered trademarks of Berrett-Koehler Publishers, Inc.

Printed in the United States of America

Berrett-Koehler books are printed on long-lasting acid-free paper. When it is available, we choose paper that has been manufactured by environmentally responsible processes. These may include using trees grown in sustainable forests, incorporating recycled paper, minimizing chlorine in bleaching, or recycling the energy produced at the paper mill.

Library of Congress Cataloging-in-Publication Data

Names: Zheng, Lily, author.
Title: Reconstructing DEI : a practitioner's workbook / Lily Zheng.
Description: First edition. | Oakland, CA : Berrett-Koehler Publishers, 2024. | Includes index.
Identifiers: LCCN 2023021042 (print) | LCCN 2023021043 (ebook) | ISBN 9781523006069 (paperback) | ISBN 9781523006076 (pdf) | ISBN 9781523006083 (epub)
Subjects: LCSH: Diversity in the workplace. | Racism in the workplace. | Discrimination in employment. | Multiculturalism. | Equality.
Classification: LCC HF5549.5.M5 Z4593 2024 (print) | LCC HF5549.5.M5 (ebook) | DDC 658.3008—dc23/eng/20220511
LC record available at https://lccn.loc.gov/2023021042
LC ebook record available at https://lccn.loc.gov/2023021043

First Edition
31 30 29 28 27 26 25 24 23
10 9 8 7 6 5 4 3 2 1

Book production: BookMatters / David Peattie
Cover and interior design: Frances Baca
Illustrations: Mark Oehlschlager
Author photograph © Richard DeVaul

To every leader, practitioner, and do-er for whom the promise of a better world outweighs the comfort of our status quo.
May we build and rebuild that world together, one organization at a time.

Contents

Introduction

When I was first imagining this workbook, the vision in my head was of a companion workbook to *DEI Deconstructed: Your No-Nonsense Guide to Doing the Work and Doing It Right.* I hoped to pull out the key exercises, recontextualize them with some new insights, and put them back out into the world in a new format. Very quickly, I realized that I didn't want to publish a book like that.

See, the most common comment I received about *DEI Deconstructed* went something like this: "Lily, now my book club and I *know* a lot more about DEI. But where do we go from here if we want to *do* it?" I realized from these comments that one of my driving goals for *DEI Deconstructed*—spurring people to take effective action immediately upon completing the book—wasn't yet achieved. I made the decision to ensure that this book was less a recapitulation of its source material, and instead an ambitious push to realize that original goal. *Reconstructing DEI: A Practitioner's Workbook*, is as much a successor and sequel to *DEI Deconstructed* as it is a companion workbook. Its purpose is simple: to guide folks to *do* DEI with the same rigor that its precursor taught them to *know* it.

Underlying everything in this book is the simple belief that everyone can learn to do effective DEI work, and the assertion that the skills required to become a DEI practitioner or an inclusive leader can be distilled, demystified, and democratized.

Despite the commonly used quip that "DEI is a lifelong journey," I wanted to map out in no uncertain detail exactly how to reach the first important milestones, and how to overcome the first few common hurdles.

The leaders and organizations I work with have asked me for this kind of guidance for years. Senior leaders come to me asking me for basic emotional intelligence skills. DEI practitioners ask for tools to better set boundaries. Employee resource groups need help organizing themselves. Middle managers want to better steward inclusive culture. As a practitioner myself, I have never been a deep expert in any one of these topics— you'll note that each one of the exercises in this book could have easily been an entire course, yearlong workshop series, or program, and for those looking for more, know that I fully expect you to dive deeper into the learning you need. But these activities were specifically chosen, and in most cases uniquely designed or adapted from my own practice, because they're the most precise, no-nonsense, and effective ways I've found in my nearly 10 years of experience doing DEI work to achieve the outcomes we seek in ourselves, those we work with, and our organizations.

They're the activities I wish I could have had as I prepared to enter the industry as a new practitioner, and the activities that I wish I could have recommended to the many leaders who have worked with me over the years.

This book is the compendium of basic tools that I expect every practitioner, inclusive leader, and advocate to know how to use before they want to further specialize, or take on the harder stuff. This book is also a DIY resource that those without any formal training can use to tackle the small problems you find every day in your organizations on your own. I believe in learning by doing, and this book is squarely about "doing." It's not a reference or a handbook—*DEI Deconstructed* was those things—but instead a guided field test using the core principles explained in *DEI Deconstructed* as a foundation.

By the time you complete this workbook, you'll have grounded yourself as a practitioner in who you are, why you do DEI work, and how you aim to focus your impact. You'll have honed your skills in organizational analysis, personal reflection, interpersonal advocacy, inclusive leadership, and conflict resolution—the skills that form the core of oucomes-centered DEI. You'll have gained valuable experience thinking and acting with outcomes and effectiveness in mind within the DEI work you do, and created a personal and professional infrastructure to do so effectively. You'll have built the core competencies required for impactful DEI work—diagnosing inequity, working with relevant parties, building movements, creating psychological safety, stewarding inclusive cultures, resolving conflict and harm, and achieving systems change, among others—and understand how to put these skills into action in your own organization.

This isn't just the book that will teach you how to "think" about changing your organization. This is the book you keep on you while you do it.

WHO AM I?

I'm a DEI practitioner and strategist with a decade's worth of experience advocating for, designing, and achieving change in dozens of organizations around the world. I'm unashamedly *also* one of the biggest critics of the DEI industry. At a time when so many organizations want Band-Aid "solutions" to enormous societal problems and so many practitioners are willing to provide them, I believe staunchly in a better future for DEI driven by practitioners willing to hold organizations accountable, equipped with the tools, practices, and skills to do so.

WHO IS THIS FOR?

Reconstructing DEI is for practitioners: anyone who is doing, or seeks to be doing, effective, pragmatic DEI work that works, and achieving the outcomes of diversity, equity, and inclusion in their own environments. New and veteran DEI professionals are of course included in this group, but I wrote this book also for the middle manager wanting to rise to the challenge of managing their diverse and distributed team, the senior leader looking to demonstrate their commitment to DEI outcomes with action, and the DEI committee member or employee resource group member wanting to use their time and energy tactically and practically. If you are a "do-er," and prepared for a boot camp that will allow you to achieve diversity, equity, and inclusion as outcomes through your own efforts, this book is for you.

How to Use This Workbook

Read *DEI Deconstructed*, or at the very least other comprehensive DEI-related books and resources, first. I'm serious. Unless you ground your learning with the prerequisite knowledge about what modern DEI work is, what it sets out to achieve, and the many ways it can fail despite the best of intentions, trying to "skip to the fun stuff" is risky and irresponsible. Enthusiasm is good! But rushing to cram tools into your toolbox without learning how to use them properly is a recipe for disaster, and sets you up as an aspiring practitioner to do harm to the very communities you're trying to serve.

Finished digesting *DEI Deconstructed* and looking for the next stage in your learning? Read on.

This workbook is split into three parts that embody a "self to systems" approach. Part 1: Self Work is focused on self-awareness. Part 2: Hone Your Skills is focused on specific skills that I believe all effective outcomes-centric practitioners must know. Part 3: Achieve Outcomes focuses on the tools of systemic change.

This workbook's exercises are ordered to progressively build on each other in chronological order. Throughout the three parts, the exercises become not only more challenging and complex, but also increasingly interdependent: while every exercise can be engaged with by individuals, the further they go in the workbook—especially in Part 3—the more valuable practitioners and leaders will find it to tackle the exercises as a group.

Each exercise will be prefaced with my tips and recommendations on how to best utilize it and the learning goals of the activity. The exercises themselves will vary, but you can expect to be spending ample time brainstorming, reflecting, and diagramming throughout this book.

At the end of this workbook, you'll find multiple roadmaps or "mini-courses" with my recommendations for sets of exercises to explore as part of a more curated learning sprint.

Keep in mind that this is a workbook, not a certification or a trophy. The exercises in this book are intended to rapidly accelerate your own DEI learning journey as a practitioner, and are intended to supplement the critical knowledge you'll gain from *DEI Deconstructed*, but the end of this book should not be your final destination. I urge you to engage with these exercises in good faith and with a critical eye, to extend graciousness to both the text and yourself for imperfections, and to commit—right here, and right now—to building on these exercises with your own thoughtful additions as you chart your own path forward in this work. I wrote this workbook as more than a one-time read, as well. The exercises I chose are evergreen resources for you to dip back into again and again to recharge your tank, recalibrate your efforts toward greater efficacy, and hold yourself accountable for being the practitioner you want to be. I'm honored that you've chosen to include this book in your journey.

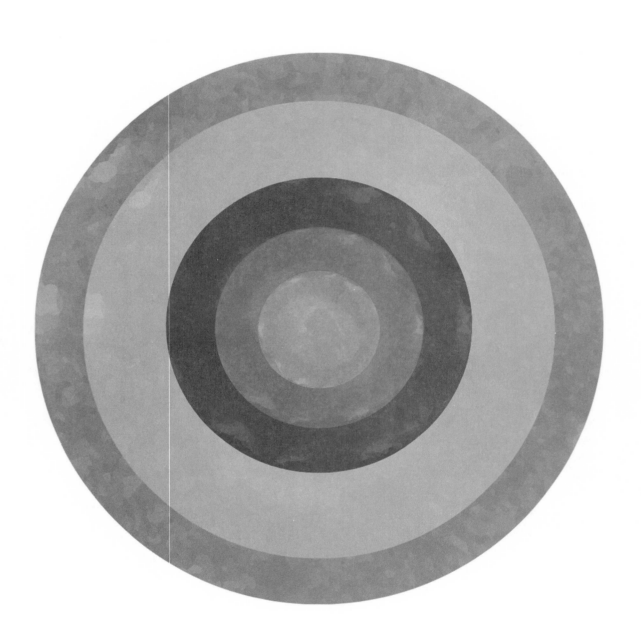

PART ONE
Self Work

UNDERSTAND YOURSELF

Those of us seeking to become or improve as DEI practitioners, inclusive leaders, and effective advocates may feel tempted to jump straight into a list of best practices. But creating the impact we seek requires more than just doing the right things, but also *being* right with ourselves—because skipping this step can result in avoidable harm to ourselves and those we're working to benefit.

> " WORKING FROM A PLACE OF KNOWING WHO WE ARE AND WHERE WE COME FROM IS, IN MY EXPERIENCE, ONE OF THE MOST POWERFUL WAYS TO GROUND OUR EFFORTS.

I've seen practitioners inflict moral injury[1] and burnout on themselves, by only realizing that the work they've chosen to do compromises their value system after agreeing to take it on; make beginner's missteps that compromise their impact, due to not unpacking their own privilege or positionality before engaging with marginalized communities; and even cause damage to organizations by acting out of unhealed trauma, rather than centering the communities they're working on behalf of.

Self-awareness and understanding help protect against this. They help us as practitioners push back against work that compromises our values, know our lane when it comes to complex issues of identity, and pursue our own healing outside of our work so we can work more sustainably and healthily.

Building self-awareness can also help us discover and rediscover our own power and expertise. Working from a place of knowing who we are and where we come from is, in my experience, one of the most powerful ways to ground our efforts. It's a fitting foundation for the work we'll be doing together in this book.

---

1. The Moral Injury Project. "What Is Moral Injury." What Is Moral Injury, July 5, 2017. https://moralinjuryproject.syr .edu/about-moral-injury.

1

Establish Your Values

UNDERSTAND YOURSELF

EXPAND YOUR CAPACITY

RELY ON OTHERS

FIND YOUR PLACE

DIAGNOSE INEQUITY

CHAMPION INCLUSION

ADDRESS CONFLICT AND HARM

ORGANIZE A MOVEMENT

REIMAGINE SYSTEMS

ACHIEVE DEI

Personal values are the guiding priorities in our lives that together make up our moral code and sense of self. The values that are most important to us are those that, if our thoughts and actions align with them, make us feel a sense of purpose and fulfillment, and if our thoughts and actions are unaligned with them, make us feel a sense of directionlessness, dissatisfaction, and even distress.

For DEI practitioners, values can feel like a pretty granular place to start. But look more closely at the choices that practitioners make, and you'll find that values are often at their heart. Many of us leave jobs because we're asked to compromise our values at work. Many of us choose the employers, industries, and even the careers we do because we're looking to follow our core values. The scary thing? While many of our values stay consistent, our values can and often do change throughout our lives.[2] Being able to name and recognize our values—especially if they've changed since we've last thought explicitly about them—helps us track what matters most to us, guide the choices we make every day, and remind us who we are no matter what situations we find ourselves in.

PRACTITIONER'S TIP

One of the underappreciated benefits of exploring your values is that it can increase your receptiveness to new, and potentially challenging, information. Even the simple task of quickly jotting down a list of your values, an exercise called a "values affirmation," has been shown to increase our ability to take constructive criticism and resist defensiveness.[3] Consider revisiting this exercise whenever you're about to go into a tough situation, to get a quick dose of fortitude.

LEARNING GOALS

- Identify your eight core values, and explore how they might show up (or not) in your life.
- Be able to fluently articulate your own values, and connect them to your day-to-day behaviors.
- Reflect on and document how your values may have evolved or changed over time.

INSTRUCTIONS

Read the following list of 60 common values. Out of all of them, circle or mark the eight core values that you think *best define who you are*. List them in any order in the My Eight Core Values chart, and for each, share some thoughts on how this value shows up in your life in your thoughts and behaviors. Afterwards, answer the reflection questions.

Acceptance To be welcomed as I am	**Accuracy** To be correct and precise in my opinions and actions	**Achievement** To accomplish valuable goals	**Adventure** To have new and exciting experiences
Attractiveness To feel and be seen as physically attractive	**Authenticity** To behave in a manner that is true to who I am	**Authority** To be in charge of others	**Autonomy** To be independent and self-determining
Beauty To appreciate and be surrounded by beautiful things	**Comfort** To have a pleasant, enjoyable life	**Compassion** To feel and show concern for others	**Contribution** To meaningfully benefit or add to society
Courage To be strong and take action in the face of fear, pain, or grief	**Creativity** To have new and original ideas and create new things	**Dependability** To be reliable and trustworthy	**Duty** To carry out my responsibility to people and society
Ecology To live in harmony with and protect the environment	**Faith** To have a strong belief in God or the doctrines of religion	**Fame** To be known and recognized	**Family** To have a happy, loving family
Flexibility To adjust to new or changing situations easily	**Forgiveness** To be compassionate to those who have harmed me or others	**Friendship** To have close, supportive friendship and companionship	**Fun** To have experiences of play, amusement, and enjoyment
Generosity To give what I have to others	**Gratitude** To readily show appreciation for and return kindness	**Growth** To continually be changing	**Honesty** To be truthful and genuine
Humility To be modest and unassuming	**Humor** To see the humorous side of myself and the world	**Industry** To work hard and well at my life tasks	**Integrity** To live consistently by a set of personal principles
Intimacy To share my innermost experience with others	**Justice** To promote equal and fair treatment for all	**Knowledge** To learn and possess valuable knowledge	**Logic** To live rationally and sensibly
Love To give love to others and be loved	**Loyalty** To provide strong support for a long period	**Mastery** To attain a high level of competence in my chosen activities	**Moderation** To avoid excess and find a middle ground

Orderliness To have a life that is well organized	Peace To seek personal peace and peace in the world	Pleasure To seek and have experiences that feel good	Popularity To be well-liked by many people
Power To have influence or control over the outcomes I desire	Purpose To have meaning and direction in life	Responsibility To make and carry out important decisions	Safety To be physically safe and secure
Self-Control To be disciplined and govern my own activities	Self-Esteem To feel positive about myself	Self-Knowledge To have a deep understanding of myself	Service To be of service to others
Sexuality To have fulfilling sexual relationships with others	Simplicity To live life simply and minimally	Spirituality To seek and find connection to something bigger than myself	Stability To have a life that stays consistent
Strength To be physically and emotionally strong and enduring	Tolerance To accept and respect those different from me	Uniqueness To be seen as remarkable, special, or unusual	Wealth To have plenty of money

MY EIGHT CORE VALUES	THIS VALUE SHOWS UP IN MY LIFE WHEN I
1. ~~Adventure~~ Acceptance	~~Take on or experience new & exciting experiences~~
2. ~~Authenticity~~ Love	Am welcome and feel like I can be true to who I am
3. Compassion	Am able to feel and show concern / care for others
4. Contribution	Can meaningfully benefit or add to society
5. Gratitude	Readily show appreciation & return kindness
6. Ecology	Life in harmony with & protect the environment
7. Peace	Seek personal peace & peace in the world
8. Pleasure	Seek & have experiences that feel good

UNDERSTAND YOURSELF

EXPAND YOUR CAPACITY

RELY ON OTHERS

FIND YOUR PLACE

DIAGNOSE INEQUITY

CHAMPION INCLUSION

ADDRESS CONFLICT AND HARM

ORGANIZE A MOVEMENT

REIMAGINE SYSTEMS

ACHIEVE DEI

REFLECTION QUESTIONS

1. How have your values influenced your life decisions? Think about your friends and family, career, education, intimate relationships, and any other important decisions you may have made.

_____

_____

_____

_____

2. How have your values changed over time, and why did they change? How easy or hard was it to notice when your values had changed?

_____

_____

_____

_____

3a. Name an action you took in the last week that embodied one or more of your current core values. How did you feel after taking it, and why?

_____

_____

_____

3b. For the action you named, what circumstances made it _easier_ to practice your values?

_____

_____

_____

_____

4a. Name an action you took in the last week that contradicted some of your values. How did you feel after taking it, and why?

_____

_____

_____

_____

4b. For the action you named, what circumstances made it _harder_ to practice your values?

_____

_____

_____

5. Given these reflections, what changes can you make in your habits and behaviors to better embody or practice your core eight values going forward?

_____

_____

_____

_____

NOTES

2. Foad, Colin M. G., Gregory G. R. Maio, and Paul H. P. Hanel. "Perceptions of values over time and why they matter." _Journal of Personality_ 89, no. 4 (2021): 689–705. https://doi.org/10.1111/jopy.12608.

3. Crocker, Jennifer, Yu Niiya, and Dominik Mischkowski. "Why does writing about important values reduce defensiveness? Self-affirmation and the role of positive other-directed feelings." _Psychological Science_ 19, no. 7 (2008): 740–747. https://doi.org/10.1111/j.1467-9280.2008.02150.x.

UNDERSTAND YOURSELF

EXPAND YOUR CAPACITY

RELY ON OTHERS

FIND YOUR PLACE

DIAGNOSE INEQUITY

CHAMPION INCLUSION

ADDRESS CONFLICT AND HARM

ORGANIZE A MOVEMENT

REIMAGINE SYSTEMS

ACHIEVE DEI

2

Claim Identity

UNDERSTAND YOURSELF

EXPAND YOUR CAPACITY

RELY ON OTHERS

FIND YOUR PLACE

DIAGNOSE INEQUITY

CHAMPION INCLUSION

ADDRESS CONFLICT AND HARM

ORGANIZE A MOVEMENT

REIMAGINE SYSTEMS

ACHIEVE DEI

Everyone has a relationship to social identities: race, gender, age/generation, ability, sexuality, class, religion, nationality, and much more. These identities do more than just connect us with other similar people; they also impact our experiences in the world, whether or not we're aware of it. Some identities are *marginalized*—associated with typically more negative experiences. Other identities are *privileged*—associated with typically more positive experiences.

Our identities don't exist separate from each other, or in a vacuum. We often experience multiple identities simultaneously, and we can be treated differently on the basis of multiple identities at once. For example, Black women don't just have the experiences of being Black added to the experiences of being a woman, but have unique experiences at the intersection of Blackness and womanhood deserving of deeper analysis. This is the concept of **intersectionality**, an analytic perspective developed by race scholar Kimberlé Crenshaw that lets us examine the various interlocking parts of our identities simultaneously.[4] Because our unique combination of identities strongly influences how we navigate and experience the world, the more we can analyze the role our many identities play in concert with each other, the better we can understand the world around us and our place within it.

PRACTITIONER'S TIP

A common experience is finding it much harder to reflect on privileged identities, compared to marginalized ones. Feeling some amount of emotion or resistance is normal! You may think at some point, "I don't have privileges; I had to work hard to earn what I have." Recognize that this exercise isn't about your effort or hard work, but instead about documenting the headwinds and tailwinds in our lives making things harder or easier for us, respectively. Use this exercise when you're looking to zoom out a bit from your day-to-day for a different perspective on your own experiences, challenges, and successes.

LEARNING GOALS

- Name your own identities across some of the most common identity dimensions, and identify which are relatively privileged vs. relatively marginalized.
- Connect your understanding of your identity intersections to your unique life experiences.
- Build fluency with using privilege and marginalization as tools to analyze your day-to-day.

INSTRUCTIONS

Review the intersectionality graphic,[5] and fill in the chart with your own identities. A list of example identities is included if you need inspiration. Once you've finished, answer the reflection questions.

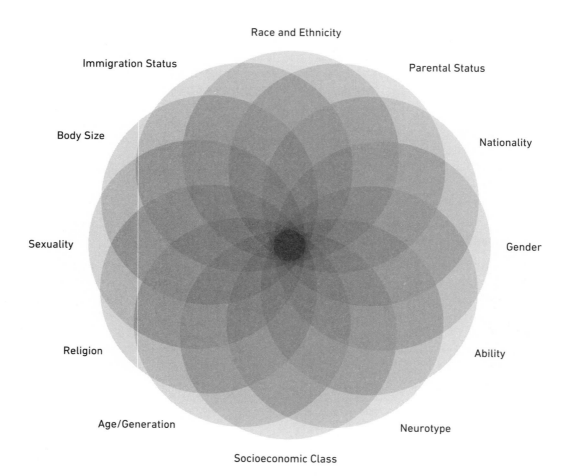

Race and Ethnicity

Immigration Status

Parental Status

Body Size

Nationality

Sexuality

Gender

Religion

Ability

Age/Generation

Neurotype

Socioeconomic Class

"Intersectionality is a lens through which you can see where power comes and collides. Where it locks and intersects. It is the acknowledgment that everyone has their own unique experiences of discrimination and privilege." —KIMBERLÉ CRENSHAW

TYPE OF IDENTITY	DEFINITION	EXAMPLES	YOUR IDENTITIES
Race and ethnicity	Social groupings related to shared physical and cultural traits	Black, White, Asian, Indigenous, Latine, Yoruba, Arab, Han Chinese, Romani	
Parental status	Whether you have or parent a child or children	Partnered vs. single parent, adoptive parent, guardian, nonparent	
Nationality	The nation you belong to or originate from	Guatemalan, Chinese, Thai, Pakistani, British, Samoan, Italian, Kenyan, American	
Gender	Your innate sense of your gender and what it means to you	Cisgender man, cisgender woman, transgender man, transgender woman, nonbinary, genderqueer	
Ability	Your cognitive, social-emotional, and physical ability to perform tasks and navigate the world	Nondisabled, deaf/hard of hearing, vision impaired, chronic pain, learning disability, physical disability	
Neurotype	The way you think, learn, and communicate compared to "normal"	Neurotypical, neurodivergent, autistic, ADHD, dyslexia, dyscalculia	
Socioeconomic class	Social grouping related to economic status	Upper, upper-middle, middle, working, lower	
Age/generation	The length of time you have lived or your generational cohort	(In the US) baby boomer, Gen X, millennial, Gen Z, Gen Alpha	
Religion	Your system of faith, belief, and worship	Christian, Muslim, Jewish, Hindu, Buddhist, nonreligious	
Sexuality	Your relationship to intimate attraction and expression	Heterosexual, gay, bisexual, queer, asexual, pansexual	
Body size	Social grouping related to your physical traits	Tall, short, fat, skinny, larger-bodied	
Immigration status	Related to your immigration generation	First-, second-, or third-generation; nonimmigrant	
Another identity important to you	Name a social identity not on this list important to your self-definition!	Veteran status, region, education, occupation, first language, etc.	

UNDERSTAND YOURSELF

EXPAND YOUR CAPACITY

RELY ON OTHERS

FIND YOUR PLACE

DIAGNOSE INEQUITY

CHAMPION INCLUSION

ADDRESS CONFLICT AND HARM

ORGANIZE A MOVEMENT

REIMAGINE SYSTEMS

ACHIEVE DEI

REFLECTION QUESTIONS

1. Of the 13 dimensions of identity shown on the graphic and in the chart, some may on average confer you advantages or disadvantages in your society or organization. Which of your identities are relatively *marginalized*? Which are relatively *privileged*?

Marginalized Identities

Privileged Identities

2. Thinking about your marginalized identities, how have they impacted your life experiences overall? What are some unique barriers you might have faced due to these identities?

3. Thinking about your privileged identities, how have they impacted your life experiences overall? What are some unique advantages you might have faced due to these identities?

4. Pick two of your marginalized identities, if applicable. How might these identities have *both* simultaneously contributed to a unique barrier or disadvantage you faced?

5. Pick two of your privileged identities, if applicable. How might these identities have *both* simultaneously contributed to a unique advantage you experienced?

6. Think about your work (including non-DEI-related work). How do your identities impact how you perceive your work and are perceived by others while working?

NOTES

4. National Association of Independent Schools. "Kimberlé Crenshaw: What Is Intersectionality?" YouTube, June 22, 2018. https://www.youtube.com/watch?v=ViDtnfQ9FHc.

5. "Intersectionality." *Instagram*. August 9, 2020. Accessed May 23, 2023. https://www.instagram.com/p/CDrJDbHBdaw/.

3

Center Your Expertise

UNDERSTAND YOURSELF

EXPAND YOUR CAPACITY

RELY ON OTHERS

FIND YOUR PLACE

DIAGNOSE INEQUITY

CHAMPION INCLUSION

ADDRESS CONFLICT AND HARM

ORGANIZE A MOVEMENT

REIMAGINE SYSTEMS

ACHIEVE DEI

Our combination of identities gives us a unique perspective on the world; going further, by dint of these identities, we can even think of ourselves as *experts* when it comes to certain topics. Your unique mix of identities as a disabled, transgender person who menstruates, for example, might make you an expert on aspects of the US medical system due to how many times you've engaged with it. Your unique mix of identities as an upper-middle class White man with an Ivy League education, for example, might make you an expert on navigating predominantly White workplace environments due to your experience in similar contexts.

Our identities by definition make us experts—but because our identities are unique, so too is our expertise limited. Understanding the gaps in our knowledge and experience helps us practice humility and curiosity, and effectively seek out the expertise of those with other experiences to gain a more complete understanding of our society.

PRACTITIONER'S TIP

Expertise can be a double-edged sword, especially if it's related to identity. The biggest risk is a cognitive bias called the "curse of knowledge" or the "curse of expertise": the assumption that other people have the same background knowledge to understand things that seem obvious to us as experts.[6] As a result of this bias, identity-related conversations can end in frustration when we realize the hard way that what feels like the most basic or obvious of observations to some ("this process is racist!" or "utilizing this resource is easy!") may feel incomprehensible to others. This exercise is about slowing down and practicing articulating not only your own expertise but also your personal gaps in knowledge. Revisit it when you're preparing for a conversation about identity with someone very different from you.

LEARNING GOALS

- Connect your most salient social identities to discrete topics of expertise and experience.
- Acknowledge gaps in your expertise related to identities you do not possess.
- Practice communicating identity-related expertise by drawing on life experience.

INSTRUCTIONS

Answer the exercise questions to outline and reflect on your own identity-related expertise. If you're looking for a challenge at the end of the exercise, draw on your answers to develop a short lecture or presentation on your expertise to deliver to a friend or colleague.

1. List up to four social identities that you would say collectively have the *largest bearing* on your everyday experiences. For examples of social identity, refer to Exercise 2: Claim Identity. For each, circle whether the identity is relatively privileged, relatively marginalized, or neither—for example: upper-middle class (privileged), queer and transgender (marginalized), neurodivergent/autistic (marginalized), DEI consultant (neither).

1.	**Privileged**	**Marginalized**	**Neither**
2.	**Privileged**	**Marginalized**	**Neither**
3.	**Privileged**	**Marginalized**	**Neither**
4.	**Privileged**	**Marginalized**	**Neither**

2. For each identity you listed, list at least one *environment or community* that you are more comfortable navigating and one that you are less comfortable navigating due to your identity—for example: *nice restaurants, rural environments; online queer and trans communities, traditional weddings; niche interest communities, extended social gatherings; corporate workplaces, employee-organized communities, unions.*

COMFORTABLE	LESS COMFORTABLE
1.	1.
2.	2.
3.	3.
4.	4.

3. For each identity you listed, list at least one topic that you have more expertise about and one topic that you have less expertise about due to having that identity (and not others)—for example: graduate school systems, unemployment and SNAP program; history of queer and trans movements, traditional heterosexual dating; double empathy problem, implied communication norms; DEI in the workplace, long-term workplace politics.

MORE EXPERTISE	LESS EXPERTISE
1.	1.
2.	2.
3.	3.
4.	4.

4. Drawing from your answers to questions 1–3, if you had to give a 10-minute presentation on a topic you have identity-related expertise with, what would you choose?

5. Try to put yourself in the shoes of someone very different from you hearing your presentation. What aspects of your presentation would be most novel to those without your identity?

UNDERSTAND YOURSELF

EXPAND YOUR CAPACITY

RELY ON OTHERS

FIND YOUR PLACE

DIAGNOSE INEQUITY

CHAMPION INCLUSION

ADDRESS CONFLICT AND HARM

ORGANIZE A MOVEMENT

REIMAGINE SYSTEMS

ACHIEVE DEI

6. Think of the same topic but presented by someone with entirely different identities from you, with different privileges and different marginalizations. How do you imagine their presentation might differ? Why?

_____

_____

_____

_____

7. If you could request a 10-minute presentation from another person on a topic you _lack_ identity-related expertise with, what would you choose?

_____

_____

_____

_____

8. What aspects of that presentation would you be hoping to learn more about; what would be most novel or interesting to you?

_____

_____

_____

_____

9. Finally, think about your own organization or community. If you were to sum up your identity-related expertise related to that organization, how would you describe it?

_____

_____

_____

_____

10. If you were to sum up the gaps in your identity-related expertise related to that organization or community, how would you describe them?

_____

_____

_____

_____

BONUS EXERCISE: PRESENT YOUR EXPERTISE

Plan out and actually deliver a 10-minute presentation on your identity-related expertise for a friend or colleague interested in hearing it, building on your previous answers to questions 1–10. Then, reflect on the following questions:

- What did you feel more or less comfortable with during your presentation?
- How was it received? To what extent did your audience learn something new?
- How might you improve that presentation if you were to deliver it again?

NOTE

6. "Curse of Knowledge." The Decision Lab, July 17, 2021. https://thedecisionlab.com/reference-guide/management/curse-of-knowledge.

UNDERSTAND YOURSELF

EXPAND YOUR CAPACITY

RELY ON OTHERS

FIND YOUR PLACE

DIAGNOSE INEQUITY

CHAMPION INCLUSION

ADDRESS CONFLICT AND HARM

ORGANIZE A MOVEMENT

REIMAGINE SYSTEMS

ACHIEVE DEI

4

Unpack Your Experiences

All of us have experienced hardship throughout our lives. Whether intense one-time events; repeated harm lasting weeks, months, or years; or even experiences of discrimination, violence, or oppression occurring over generations, hardship often sticks with us in some form or another. For many of us, especially those with one or more marginalized social identities, that hardship has had a significant bearing on the person we are today. These experiences aren't good or bad—they simply are. Yet, how we internalize and respond to these experiences has bearing on our efficacy as DEI practitioners.

On the one extreme, living in a constant state of emotional activation tied to our hardship or trauma can be dangerous.[7]

We may inadvertently prioritize unmet needs in ourselves, rather than centering the communities and organizations we are working to benefit, and as a result do harm. On the other extreme, trying to act like the hardship we experienced never happened can be equally harmful. Repressing our triggers and working without attending to ourselves can result in long-term burnout, compassion fatigue, and diminished impact.[8] Naming our experiences—even traumatic ones— without judgment and tying them to who we are today can help us start unpacking what we're each bringing to the DEI work we do.

PRACTITIONER'S TIP

This exercise is a deeply personal self-examination. Utilize it when you're looking for insight into or a reminder of your own life experiences below the surface, and as part of a process of recalibrating your overall reason and approach to DEI work.

Reflecting on hardship, especially traumatic experiences, can be a taxing experience for anybody. Ensure that you feel physically and mentally prepared for potentially difficult emotions to surface during the exercise before beginning, and give yourself permission to pause or skip the activity if you're feeling overwhelmed. During the exercise, if you find yourself needing to relax, consider utilizing deep breathing or paired muscle relaxation (tightening, then relaxing them), engaging in physical movement, splashing your face with cold water, or otherwise utilizing what are called "distress tolerance skills."[9] If you're finding that this exercise is bringing up more intense emotions than you can tolerate, consider reaching out to a mental health professional to continue processing these experiences with more formal support and guidance.

LEARNING GOALS

- Name and reflect on your experiences of hardship and trauma.
- Reflect on how your hardship and trauma affect your thoughts and behaviors, and list your present-day triggers.
- Describe how greater awareness of hardship and trauma might benefit your DEI work.

UNDERSTAND YOURSELF

EXPAND YOUR CAPACITY

RELY ON OTHERS

FIND YOUR PLACE

DIAGNOSE INEQUITY

CHAMPION INCLUSION

ADDRESS CONFLICT AND HARM

ORGANIZE A MOVEMENT

REIMAGINE SYSTEMS

ACHIEVE DEI

INSTRUCTIONS

The following chart lists different types of hardship and trauma by category: acute, chronic, complex, and historical. Fill out the chart with examples of your own experiences of hardship or trauma, if any, then answer the reflection questions. Remember to stay in touch with your emotions as you fill this chart out, taking breaks as needed. It's okay if you choose not to write down all of your experiences, and also okay if you don't have any experiences of hardship or trauma in one or more categories.

CATEGORY	DEFINITION	EXAMPLES	YOUR EXPERIENCES
Acute	A single, isolated incident	▪ Natural disasters ▪ Single acts of violence or terrorism ▪ Sudden unexpected losses (of loved ones, relationships, possessions, ability, etc.)	
Chronic	Experiences that are repeated and prolonged	▪ Prolonged family or community violence ▪ Long-term illness ▪ Chronic bullying ▪ Chronic poverty ▪ Repeated discrimination ▪ Repeated exposure to loss and grief	
Complex	Traumatic experiences, often at an early age, involving the feeling of powerlessness	▪ Physical, emotional, and/or sexual abuse ▪ Neglect or abandonment ▪ Witnessing domestic violence ▪ Human trafficking ▪ Living in a war zone	
Historical	Collective experiences shared by a cultural group across generations	▪ Generational trauma from war, displacement, and violence ▪ Systemic racism ▪ Colonization/imperialism ▪ Genocide/ethnic cleansing	

REFLECTION QUESTIONS

1. What was the hardest part of this exercise for you? What emotions came up, if any?

_____

_____

_____

_____

2. In what ways have your *acute* experiences of hardship or trauma shaped who you are today? Consider your behaviors, habits, preferences, lifestyle, and relationships. You can skip this question if you did not list any acute experiences.

_____

_____

_____

3. In what ways have your *chronic* experiences of hardship or trauma shaped who you are today? You can skip this question if you did not list any chronic experiences.

_____

_____

_____

4. In what ways have your *complex* experiences of hardship or trauma shaped who you are today? You can skip this question if you did not list any complex experiences.

_____

_____

_____

UNDERSTAND YOURSELF

EXPAND YOUR CAPACITY

RELY ON OTHERS

FIND YOUR PLACE

DIAGNOSE INEQUITY

CHAMPION INCLUSION

ADDRESS CONFLICT AND HARM

ORGANIZE A MOVEMENT

REIMAGINE SYSTEMS

ACHIEVE DEI

5. In what ways have your *historical* experiences of hardship or trauma shaped who you are today? You can skip this question if you did not list any historical experiences.

_____

_____

_____

6. How do your experiences shape your approach to work, especially DEI-related work? What new insights or thoughts emerge after making these connections?

_____

_____

_____

7. What triggers—things that cause painful memories or emotions to surface—might you have related to your experiences? How do you or might you manage these triggers in your work?

_____

_____

_____

8. How might unpacking personal experiences of hardship and trauma be useful for your own DEI work? List potential benefits of doing so, and potential risks to be managed.

_____

_____

_____

NOTES

7. Chin, Dorothy, Amber M. Smith-Clapham, and Gail E. Wyatt. "Race-based trauma and post-traumatic growth through identity transformation." *Frontiers in Psychology* 14 (2023). https://doi.org/10.3389/fpsyg.2023.1031602.

8. Newell, Jason M., and Gordon A. MacNeil. "Professional burnout, vicarious trauma, secondary traumatic stress, and compassion fatigue." *Best Practices in Mental Health* 6, no. 2 (2010): 57–68.

9. Compitus, Katherine. "What Are Distress Tolerance Skills? The Ultimate DBT Toolkit." PositivePsychology.com, March 3, 2023. https://positivepsychology.com/distress-tolerance-skills/.

" NAMING OUR EXPERIENCES—EVEN TRAUMATIC ONES—WITHOUT JUDGMENT AND TYING THEM TO WHO WE ARE TODAY CAN HELP US START UNPACKING WHAT WE'RE EACH BRINGING TO THE DEI WORK WE DO.

EXPAND YOUR CAPACITY

Gaining the self-awareness to understand who we are, what we know, and what we've experienced is a foundational prerequisite for any effective DEI work. The next step is to directly expand our capacity and capability to engage in what can often be a protracted and long-term undertaking, by working on our mindsets, our objectives, and our relationships to ourselves as practitioners.

> " WITHOUT SELF-COMPASSION ROOTED IN A CLEAR UNDERSTANDING OF WHAT WE SET OUT TO ACHIEVE, WE CAN QUICKLY FEEL OVERWHELMED.

To ensure our efforts are sustainable and fruitful, we need to ground our work in a clear purpose, a clear "why" that can serve as our moral compass in challenging times. To equip ourselves as practitioners to shape systems over the long haul, weather conflict and challenge, and retain our focus on the outcomes we're hoping to create, we need three internal skills: emotional regulation, self-compassion, and humility.

Without grounding, we can take up this work with impulsive or flimsy declarations of purpose that are so brittle that we falter upon our first setback. Having thrown ourselves into DEI without a long-term vision for achieving impact or sustaining ourselves, we can quickly burn out or become disillusioned with this work. But even with a firm grounding, lacking personal capacity will mean that we won't get far. Without emotional regulation, we'll be unmoored and unstable in our work. We'll be so affected by the volatile conversations and environments we engage with that they will quickly overwhelm our hearts, minds, and bodies. Without self-compassion rooted in a clear understanding of what we set out to achieve, we can quickly feel overwhelmed by the scale of the systems we seek to change and direct our frustration toward ourselves, rather than the obstacles that are so common in this work. And without humility, we can get ahead of ourselves, convinced that we alone will "save the world."

A common saying among DEI practitioners is that "DEI is lifelong learning." I agree, but sustaining ourselves throughout this lifelong journey is harder than sound bites make it out to be. Sustainable DEI doesn't just emerge from nowhere: it stems from a strong personal capacity to do this work, and it accordingly requires purpose, humility, regulation, and compassion, as well as the dedication to maintain them all as part of our discipline as practitioners.

5

Tune Your Compass

Practitioners have been asking and answering the question of "why" when it comes to DEI work for the greater part of 60 years, since the start of DEI work in the 1960s. But beyond cliché retorts like "it's the right thing to do" or "it makes business sense," few folks are able to fully articulate their personal reasons for engaging in DEI work beyond trite statements. Plus, even when these statements are developed—say in corporate "mission and values" sessions—they're rarely revisited. Their use is almost entirely as a fun team-building exercise, rather than as a real operational tool.

This is because it takes one more step to turn a powerful and personal "why" into a sustainable tool of DEI work: operationalizing it into a well-defined DEI compass. With this enhanced "why" grounded in tangible objectives, practitioners can use it time and time again to recenter and recalibrate our work when we're feeling lost. Tuning our DEI compass allows us to hold ourselves ethically and operationally accountable to the world we're trying to create over the long haul, especially in moments where we feel lost or demoralized.

PRACTITIONER'S TIP

It can be easy to mistakenly view this exercise as a "check the box" activity to write a one-time personal statement. However, a well-made compass for DEI work turns out to be something we as practitioners use almost all the time. When we make decisions on whether to try and fix systems from the inside or tear them down from the outside, whether to see our working with a problematic organization as being complicit or as being tactical, whether to continue doing the same work we started with or change our tactics and practices, all of this requires that we have a tool to help us make the right decision. Use this exercise to remind yourself why you do this work, before you make a hard decision, or when you need a source of accountability.

LEARNING GOALS

- Draw on your own story to describe the world you're working toward and the outcomes within it that matter to you.
- Craft a succinct and unique DEI compass based on your goals.
- Practice analyzing your own actions and their degree of alignment to your compass.

UNDERSTAND YOURSELF

EXPAND YOUR CAPACITY

RELY ON OTHERS

FIND YOUR PLACE

DIAGNOSE INEQUITY

CHAMPION INCLUSION

ADDRESS CONFLICT AND HARM

ORGANIZE A MOVEMENT

REIMAGINE SYSTEMS

ACHIEVE DEI

INSTRUCTIONS

Answer the exercise questions to describe the world you're working toward and the outcomes within it, then use your reflections to create your unique DEI compass. Afterwards, answer the reflection questions.

1. How did you come to be interested in DEI work? Share a story if applicable.

_____

_____

_____

_____

2. How does your interest in DEI work connect to the social identities most important to you? Refer back to Exercise 2: Claim Identity for inspiration.

_____

_____

_____

_____

3. Imagine that your DEI work has "fully succeeded." How would you define that success in your own context, like your team, community, or organization?

_____

_____

_____

_____

4. What are the biggest differences between that successful future and the present day?

_____

_____

_____

_____

5. Given those differences, what are the major goals you would need to achieve through your own efforts to create the future you imagine?

_____

_____

_____

_____

6. Morals describe our baseline for "right" vs. "wrong." Thinking about your own present and future DEI efforts, how would you describe your _morals_? If there was a "right" way you wanted to engage in DEI work, what would it be?

_____

_____

_____

_____

In the box, create your own DEI compass by filling in the blanks with your answers from questions 2, 3, 5, and 6. A sample DEI compass is provided.

Sample

I do DEI work as a (2) _queer, trans person of color with class privilege_ to contribute directly to a future where (3) _the organizations I work with set the standard for their industries in how diverse, equitable, and inclusive they are._ I will do my part by working toward (5) _a standard for DEI practitioners in this industry and strong accountability mechanisms for all organizations, especially corporations, that do DEI._ It's important to me that as a practitioner, I work in a way that centers my strong beliefs in (6) _impact, accountability, and humility._

UNDERSTAND YOURSELF

EXPAND YOUR CAPACITY

RELY ON OTHERS

FIND YOUR PLACE

DIAGNOSE INEQUITY

CHAMPION INCLUSION

ADDRESS CONFLICT AND HARM

ORGANIZE A MOVEMENT

REIMAGINE SYSTEMS

ACHIEVE DEI

My DEI Compass

I do DEI work as a (2)_____ to contribute directly to a

future where (3)_____

_____

_____. I will do my part by working toward (5)_____

_____

_____

_____

_____. It's important to me that as a

practitioner, I work in a way that centers my strong beliefs in (6)_____

_____

_____.

REFLECTION QUESTIONS

1. Think about a time you felt strong negative emotions like shame, guilt, sadness, grief, or regret related to DEI work or a DEI topic. What happened that made you feel this way?

_____

_____

_____

_____

2. Our DEI compass can be a useful tool to gauge and evaluate our actions. Thinking about the experience you named, was there any aspect of your DEI compass that was violated, overlooked, or devalued in the situation you experienced? If so, what aspect and why?

_____

_____

_____

_____

3. Now, think about a time you felt strong positive emotions like pride, joy, connection, or satisfaction related to DEI work or a DEI topic. What happened that made you feel this way?

_____

_____

_____

_____

4. Our DEI compass can be a useful tool to gauge and evaluate our actions. Thinking about the experience you named, was there any aspect of your DEI compass that was prioritized, centered, or valued in the situation you experienced? If so, what aspect and why?

_____

_____

_____

_____

5. Now that you've created your own DEI compass, how might you use it in the future? List a few situations where it would be valuable to you, and why.

_____

_____

_____

_____

UNDERSTAND YOURSELF

EXPAND YOUR CAPACITY

RELY ON OTHERS

FIND YOUR PLACE

DIAGNOSE INEQUITY

CHAMPION INCLUSION

ADDRESS CONFLICT AND HARM

ORGANIZE A MOVEMENT

REIMAGINE SYSTEMS

ACHIEVE DEI

6

Regulate Your Emotions

DEI work is often emotional work. Even the most procedural, bureaucratic effort to achieve change can quickly become emotional, simply because inequity and injustice affect people emotionally, and ending inequity and injustice requires attending to these emotions. Being attuned to our emotions, especially our sense of empathy, can be a superpower when it comes to DEI work. It helps us connect with others and quickly grasp the magnitude of the issues they're facing. But *too much* connection can be dangerous for practitioners, especially if we lack means to regulate our own emotional response.

If we're so attuned with people's emotions that we feel them as our own, it only takes a few people in crisis to push us into crisis ourselves.[10] As practitioners, we need to be able to strike a balance between feeling our emotions enough to connect with those we work with, and regulating them to protect ourselves and our efficacy. Building emotional regulation into our skill set increases our stamina to hold space for more intense emotions, so that we are able to sustain our work and impact through the emotional ups and downs that can occur.

PRACTITIONER'S TIP

While emotional regulation is useful for any practitioner, it's also true that the more emotionally intense the work, the more crucial emotional regulation becomes and the more techniques you'll need to know. For example, you may be able to get through a brief disagreement with deep breathing alone, but you'll need to use a greater range of techniques with greater creativity to navigate a hostile relationship. Accordingly, the "skill" required for emotional regulation isn't just in the number of techniques you know, but in deeper knowledge on when to use which techniques and the "muscle memory" of doing so born from experience. Use this exercise as a refresher and reminder of some of the most common effective techniques that exist, especially before heading into an emotionally challenging environment.

LEARNING GOALS

- Recall and reflect on your past experiences of emotional dysregulation.
- Review a range of effective emotional regulation techniques, and apply them to your own experiences.
- Create a plan for when and how you will use emotional regulation techniques.

UNDERSTAND YOURSELF

EXPAND YOUR CAPACITY

RELY ON OTHERS

FIND YOUR PLACE

DIAGNOSE INEQUITY

CHAMPION INCLUSION

ADDRESS CONFLICT AND HARM

ORGANIZE A MOVEMENT

REIMAGINE SYSTEMS

ACHIEVE DEI

INSTRUCTIONS

Answer the exercise questions, then learn about different emotional regulation techniques on the chart. Complete the chart with brainstormed scenarios of how you might have used each type of technique in a situation you experienced. Finally, answer the reflection questions.

1. Think back to the last time you felt your negative emotions, like anger, frustration, sadness, or anxiety, overwhelm or get the better of you. What happened?

_____

_____

_____

_____

2. In the situation you shared, what were some of the factors that led to you feeling overwhelmed? Describe both external factors (relating to other people, or your environment) and internal factors (related to yourself, your feelings, and your behaviors).

_____

_____

_____

_____

The chart on the opposite page lists different types of emotional regulation techniques, with examples. For each type of technique, fill out the chart with one technique you could see yourself using in the situation you described.

TYPE	DEFINITION	EXAMPLES	IN MY SITUATION I WOULD
Distancing	Putting psychological distance between ourselves and tough thoughts and emotions	▪ Imagining a hard situation from another's perspective ▪ Pausing for 10 seconds before responding to a comment ▪ Revisiting a hard memory as if viewing it on a distant screen	
Attention control	Changing the object of our attention to mitigate tough or difficult thoughts and emotions	▪ Short-term distraction by watching your favorite show or media ▪ Focusing on a positive aspect of a hard situation ▪ Focusing sustained attention on an unrelated important task	
Mindfulness	Increasing our awareness of our thoughts and emotions and accepting them as valid	▪ Naming your thoughts and emotions, even negative ones ▪ Grounding yourself with touch, hearing, sight, smell, and taste ▪ Focusing attention on your breath or a neutral object	
Taking action	Planning and executing on actions that address tough or difficult thoughts and emotions	▪ Acting opposite to your emotions (like a kind act after feeling anger, activity after feeling depression, connection after feeling shame) ▪ Intentional action to improve the situation or meet your needs	

UNDERSTAND YOURSELF

EXPAND YOUR CAPACITY

RELY ON OTHERS

FIND YOUR PLACE

DIAGNOSE INEQUITY

CHAMPION INCLUSION

ADDRESS CONFLICT AND HARM

ORGANIZE A MOVEMENT

REIMAGINE SYSTEMS

ACHIEVE DEI

REFLECTION QUESTIONS

1. What feelings came up while you were filling out the chart? Why?

2. Think about how you have typically addressed emotionally challenging experiences in the past. What, if any, emotional regulation techniques did you use? How effective were they?

3. How might emotional regulation techniques help you when it comes to DEI work? Be specific with naming a technique and a situation where it might be helpful.

4. Different people will find different techniques harder vs. easier. Which techniques on the chart feel hardest for you? Easiest?

5. Name one technique on this chart that you would like to intentionally make time to learn and build mastery in. How will you create opportunities to practice it?

6. Drawing from your answers to the chart, make a plan for the next time you end up in an emotionally challenging situation, drawing on at least two emotional regulation techniques.

NOTE

10. Hatfield, Elaine, Richard L. Rapson, and Yen-Chi L. Le. "Emotional contagion and empathy." *The Social Neuroscience of Empathy* (2011): 19.

UNDERSTAND YOURSELF

EXPAND YOUR CAPACITY

RELY ON OTHERS

FIND YOUR PLACE

DIAGNOSE INEQUITY

CHAMPION INCLUSION

ADDRESS CONFLICT AND HARM

ORGANIZE A MOVEMENT

REIMAGINE SYSTEMS

ACHIEVE DEI

7

Embrace Humility

DEI work will inevitably involve working alongside people with identities you yourself don't share and don't understand as well, and within systems that may be more or less familiar to you. While we should constantly strive to increase our *competence* in discussing and comprehending the many kinds of experiences and systems in the world around us, we are best equipped for success when we become comfortable being active and humble learners along the way.

There's no more important place to learn the practice of humility than with culture and social identity: despite the abundance of diversity in our world, for many it still feels impossibly hard to "get it right" when it comes to learning about others' cultures. But even if we struggle as learners, we can approach the same challenges from the other vantage point, as teachers. By reflecting on our own knowledge as teachers and how we might best reach beginners different from us, we can gain valuable insight into how we can embrace humility as lifelong learners.

PRACTITIONER'S TIP

"Cultural humility," a perspective and process involving lifelong learning and self-reflection on cultural knowledge, emerged in the late 90s as a critique of the idea of "cultural competence," an approach that positioned cultural knowledge as a discrete body of knowledge that one could gain mastery in.[11] Cultural humility, advocates argued, was a recognition that no two people from a culture are the same, that cultural learning never ends, and that true "competence" was never possible. This perspective is a valuable one. However, there's something to be said about the value of "competence" too—and while there's no discrete endpoint to cultural knowledge that practitioners can reach, and it's important for practitioners to avoid stereotyping individuals with information about their culture, it's very much still possible to become "more competent" about cultures and use this knowledge for good. Use this exercise to reflect on your own cultural knowledge, and revisit it over time to see how your understanding of a given culture has grown over time.

LEARNING GOALS

- Articulate the difference between "surface" and "deep" aspects of culture.
- Comprehensively name surface and deep aspects of your own culture.
- Reflect on how you might teach about your own culture and learn about others'.

INSTRUCTIONS

Read the following passage on types of culture, and review the cultural iceberg graphic. Fill in the charts with answers related to your experiences with a community or culture that you're a part of. Finally, answer the reflection questions.

Culture, Surface and Deep

Culture is the values, beliefs, communication norms, behaviors and practices, symbols, and objects that groups and communities use to define themselves as part of a collective.[12] Culture is a property of not only people grouped by social identity—race, gender, sexuality, religion, and so on—but also virtually any other kind of group, from an informal circle of friends to large multinational corporations.

While no two cultures are ever exactly the same, we can think of cultural markers as either being "surface" or being "deep."[13] Surface aspects of culture are visible and obvious. They're the things you can notice quickly upon entering a new culture: how people express themselves, the holidays they observe, the music they play, and how they greet each other, for example. Deep aspects of culture are harder to notice upon first glance and are rarely stated explicitly but are highly important: they are the part of the iceberg below the surface. They include social rules regarding manners and politeness; expectations and norms relating to social identities like race, gender, sexuality, age, and class; and common understandings of topics like justice and power.

The more we understand about culture, whether our own or that of others, the more effectively and intentionally we can navigate different cultural contexts. Being able to understand the key aspects of a culture is like being able to explain the main rules of a game. They may not cover every exception or variation, but you'll know enough to get by.

1. Name a group or community you belong to with its own unique culture. You'll be referencing this group or community in the following chart.

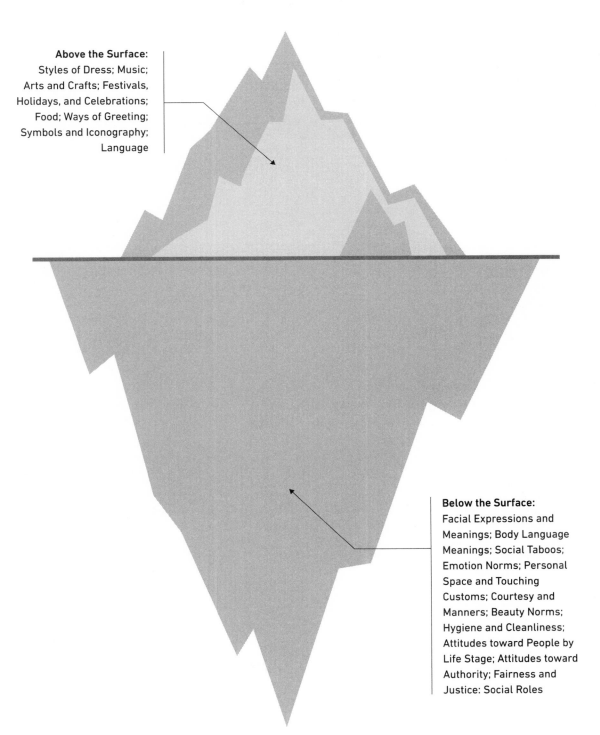

Above the Surface:
Styles of Dress; Music;
Arts and Crafts; Festivals,
Holidays, and Celebrations;
Food; Ways of Greeting;
Symbols and Iconography;
Language

Below the Surface:
Facial Expressions and
Meanings; Body Language
Meanings; Social Taboos;
Emotion Norms; Personal
Space and Touching
Customs; Courtesy and
Manners; Beauty Norms;
Hygiene and Cleanliness;
Attitudes toward People by
Life Stage; Attitudes toward
Authority; Fairness and
Justice: Social Roles

UNDERSTAND
YOURSELF

EXPAND YOUR
CAPACITY

RELY ON
OTHERS

FIND YOUR
PLACE

DIAGNOSE
INEQUITY

CHAMPION
INCLUSION

ADDRESS CONFLICT
AND HARM

ORGANIZE A
MOVEMENT

REIMAGINE
SYSTEMS

ACHIEVE
DEI

2. Thinking about the unique culture of the group or community you chose, answer the prompts to fill in the chart with examples of surface culture. Don't worry about writing the "correct" answers; your unique experience of culture may not resemble others' experiences but is always authentic to you. Additionally, it's okay to not have an answer for every box, since the culture you chose may not have substantial practices or norms different from the wider culture you're in, for that particular category.

ABOVE THE SURFACE (VISIBLE, OBVIOUS)	
Styles of Dress What clothing is important to this culture?	**Music** What music is important to this culture?
Arts and Crafts What forms of art and expression are important to this culture?	**Festivals, Holidays, and Celebrations** What important days or occasions are observed by this culture?
Food What food is important to this culture?	**Ways of Greeting** How do members of this culture greet each other?
Symbols and Iconography What visual imagery is important to this culture, and what does it mean?	**Language** What language or vocabulary is used by this culture?

3. Next, do the same for deep culture.

BELOW THE SURFACE (LESS VISIBLE, LESS OBVIOUS)	
Facial Expressions and Meanings What unique facial expressions exist, and what do they mean in this culture?	**Body Language Meanings** What unique body language exists, and what does it mean in this culture?
Social Taboos What topics or actions are considered taboo in this culture?	**Emotion Norms** What are common expectations regarding the expression of emotion in this culture?
Personal Space and Touching Customs What are common expectations regarding personal space and touch in this culture?	**Courtesy and Manners** What are common expectations regarding courtesy and "good manners" in this culture?
Beauty Norms What is considered beautiful in this culture?	**Hygiene and Cleanliness** What are common expectations regarding hygiene and cleanliness in this culture?
Attitudes toward People by Life Stage How does this culture treat adolescents, young adults, and elders?	**Attitudes toward Authority** What are the traits this culture ascribes to leaders, and how does it treat them?
Fairness and Justice What is considered fair and just in this culture?	**Social Roles (Race, Gender, Class, etc.)** How does this culture think about racial, gender, class, and other differences?

UNDERSTAND YOURSELF

EXPAND YOUR CAPACITY

RELY ON OTHERS

FIND YOUR PLACE

DIAGNOSE INEQUITY

CHAMPION INCLUSION

ADDRESS CONFLICT AND HARM

ORGANIZE A MOVEMENT

REIMAGINE SYSTEMS

ACHIEVE DEI

REFLECTION QUESTIONS

1. How was the process of filling out the chart for you? Which questions were hardest to answer?

_____

_____

_____

_____

2. Think about the elements of surface vs. deep culture you shared. How did you come to understand these things, and did you learn about them in different ways?

_____

_____

_____

_____

3. What are some of the most common misconceptions people have about your culture? How do people come by these misconceptions?

_____

_____

_____

_____

4. If someone wanted to learn more about your culture from you, what would be a _disrespectful_ way for them to engage with you?

_____

_____

_____

_____

5. If someone wanted to learn more about your culture from you, what would be a *respectful* way for them to engage with you?

6. Now think about a situation in which *you're* the person looking to learn about another culture that you don't have lived experience in, rather than the teacher. If you were trying to learn by reaching out to a person from that culture, what kinds of questions might you ask? How might you embody *humility* in your interactions?

7. Thinking about your responses to this exercise, how would you operationalize "cultural humility" as a learning practice for yourself?

NOTES

11. Tervalon, Melanie, and Jann Murray-Garcia. "Cultural humility versus cultural competence: A critical distinction in defining physician training outcomes in multicultural education." *Journal of Health Care for the Poor and Underserved* 9, no. 2 (1998): 117–125. https://doi.org/10.1353/hpu.2010.0233.

12. Cole, Nicki Lisa. "Defining Culture and Why It Matters to Sociologists." ThoughtCo, August 2, 2019. https://www.thoughtco.com/culture-definition-4135409.

13. Hall, Edward T. *Beyond Culture*. Anchor, 1976.

UNDERSTAND YOURSELF

EXPAND YOUR CAPACITY

RELY ON OTHERS

FIND YOUR PLACE

DIAGNOSE INEQUITY

CHAMPION INCLUSION

ADDRESS CONFLICT AND HARM

ORGANIZE A MOVEMENT

REIMAGINE SYSTEMS

ACHIEVE DEI

8

Extend Compassion

Many people enter DEI work out of both passion to make change and compassion toward those experiencing exclusion or inequity. To expand your capacity to do this work effectively, it's critical to center your work with a well-tuned DEI compass, learn to regulate intense emotions, and approach the work of teaching, learning, and making an impact with humility.

But even if we double, triple, or quintuple our capacity to do DEI work, each and every one of us will someday hit a wall. We may fail to make the impact we seek, even if we do everything right. We may face setbacks and adversity that pushes our ability to cope and regulate to its limit. This section's final exercise isn't meant to help you do more—it's to help you practice being kind enough to accept yourself as "good enough." Learning to practice and extend the same compassion toward ourselves as we would extend toward others is what allows us to care for ourselves so that we might sustain our work over the long haul.[14]

PRACTITIONER'S TIP

Self-compassion as a practice is often used as a remedial tool, for when practitioners are at the end of their rope or on the cusp of burnout. But waiting until there's no other option means that for many, self-compassion is only ever taken seriously when it's too late for it to help. Treating self-compassion as a regular habit, even if it seems like overdoing it in response to small setbacks, can increase our resilience and sense of balance over time. Consider revisiting this exercise whenever you're processing a tough situation, or simply as a periodic healthy practice.

LEARNING GOALS

- Reflect on how you extend compassion to those you care about.
- Practice extending that compassion to yourself.
- Identify sources of personal resistance to self-compassion without judgment.

UNDERSTAND YOURSELF

EXPAND YOUR CAPACITY

RELY ON OTHERS

FIND YOUR PLACE

DIAGNOSE INEQUITY

CHAMPION INCLUSION

ADDRESS CONFLICT AND HARM

ORGANIZE A MOVEMENT

REIMAGINE SYSTEMS

ACHIEVE DEI

INSTRUCTIONS

Fill in the left column of the following chart with examples of negative things you've heard other people say about themselves, or negative things you might have said about yourself. In the middle column, write how you might respond *compassionately* to each corresponding statement. Note that a compassionate response need not try to fix the problem, motivate people to take action, or try to inspire—simply validating the sentiment or showing empathy can be powerful. In the final column, use your compassionate response to others as inspiration to make a similar "I" statement directed at yourself. Each column begins with an example. After filling out the chart, answer the reflection questions.

NEGATIVE SELF-TALK	COMPASSIONATE RESPONSE	COMPASSIONATE "I" STATEMENT
I can't do this—it's too hard. I'm a failure.	It's okay for things to be hard, and to feel frustrated when it feels like you're not making progress. Taking a break doesn't make you a failure.	I can be frustrated at hard tasks, and I may not always be able to see the progress I'm making. Struggling with hard things and taking care of myself doesn't make me a failure.

REFLECTION QUESTIONS

1. Look at the examples of negative self-talk you listed. Are there any common patterns or themes? If so, why do you think that is?

_____

_____

_____

_____

2. Two common pitfalls to self-compassion are problem-solving (ignoring your feelings to try and immediately resolve the source) and toxic positivity (denying your feelings to try and replace them with "positive" ones, even if they don't feel authentic). If you have run into these pitfalls before, how might you maintain your commitment to self-compassion?

_____

_____

_____

_____

3. Many people find it easier to show compassion toward other people than to direct that same compassion at themselves. Which compassionate responses directed at others were hardest for you to turn into "I" statements directed at yourself?

_____

_____

_____

_____

4. Often, people can feel a sense of internal resistance or aversion to self-compassion. This may be because they feel like they don't deserve it, like it's a waste of time, or like it indicates weakness, among other reasons. If you have ever felt resistance to self-compassion, why?

_____

_____

_____

UNDERSTAND YOURSELF

EXPAND YOUR CAPACITY

RELY ON OTHERS

FIND YOUR PLACE

DIAGNOSE INEQUITY

CHAMPION INCLUSION

ADDRESS CONFLICT AND HARM

ORGANIZE A MOVEMENT

REIMAGINE SYSTEMS

ACHIEVE DEI

While this exercise focuses on compassionate self-talk, there are many other ways to practice self-compassion, including physical soothing (like gently feeling the pace of your breath), listing things you appreciate about yourself, and meeting your physical and emotional needs.

5. Beyond engaging in compassionate self-talk, what other things might you do to practice self-compassion?

_____

_____

_____

_____

6. Make a plan for the next time you experience a setback or hardship. How might you incorporate self-compassion into how you process the event?

_____

_____

_____

_____

NOTE

14. Lefebvre, Jade-Isis, Francesco Montani, and François Courcy. "Self-compassion and resilience at work: A practice-oriented review." _Advances in Developing Human Resources_ 22, no. 4 (2020): 437–452. https://doi.org/10.1177/1523422320949145.

" LEARNING TO PRACTICE AND EXTEND THE SAME COMPASSION TOWARD OURSELVES AS WE WOULD EXTEND TOWARD OTHERS IS WHAT ALLOWS US TO SUSTAIN OUR WORK OVER THE LONG HAUL.

RELY ON OTHERS

The exercises in the previous two sections, Understand Yourself and Expand Your Capacity, focused on ways we can prepare ourselves to do the work with greater self-awareness and a practitioner's capacity. But DEI work is more than just individual practitioners saving the day: the most important work not only benefits from strong interpersonal skills; it just about requires it. In this section, Rely on Others, the exercises are about building on the inner foundation you've just created to strengthen our relationships to others.

DEI work simply doesn't work if done solo. It doesn't matter how much we know or how efficiently we can work; going at enormous challenges on our own is a ticket to personal burnout and disillusionment. Without people we can turn to for support, the only way we can rest and recover from the work is to simply stop doing it. Without becoming able to comfortably ask for help or set boundaries, we won't get to choose our breaks; our bodies and minds will decide for us, and never at convenient times. And without others to hold us accountable, we run the risk of straying from the impact we hope to have.

But when we're able to rely on others, suddenly our responsibility feels less like "saving the world" and more like "doing our part." That shift itself is transformational. It lets us give radical permission to ourselves to simply be, to find joy, to rest, and to avoid infusing the same cycles of overwork, overproduction, exploitation, and burnout we're trying to end into our own DEI work.

> " CREATING A PERSONAL SUPPORT NETWORK AND COMMUNITY IS DEEPLY RELATIONAL WORK THAT ALLOWS US TO SUSTAIN OURSELVES.

Forming strong supportive relationships enables a host of benefits. Creating a personal support network and community is deeply relational work that allows us to sustain ourselves. Becoming able to ask for help and set boundaries allows us to learn, grow, and rest. Even something as basic as DEI-related accountability requires that we be comfortable working in relationship with others to succeed, simply because of how tough, if not impossible, progress is to achieve on our own.

9

Identify Your Anchors

Especially during times of hardship, and also during times of joy, reflection, and exploration, having important others around us can help us anchor ourselves and receive the guidance and support we need. These important others—our anchors—aren't just random people, and they don't always neatly line up with our friends, families, or loved ones. The most powerful anchors are those people who we trust most deeply, who share a deep sense of mutual loyalty and commitment, and often who share important core values with us. And while they can often be members of our families of origin or loved ones, they can also be chosen family, extended family members, friends, colleagues, or an eclectic mix of all of the above.

These anchors are important sources of support both within and outside of our work as practitioners. They can be thought partners, emotional support, sources of accountability, trusted advisors, and listening ears. They can help meet our deepest and most important needs, so that we feel steady and centered when doing DEI work. The more we're able to rely on a network of support, rather than only ourselves, the more sustainable our work will be.

PRACTITIONER'S TIP

Many people are familiar with the romanticized ideal of finding a single person—a "soulmate"—who meets as many of our needs as possible and serves as our sole anchor in life. In reality, this isn't a universally achievable experience or even a realistic expectation. Working instead to fully understand your needs, and building strong relationships with many people in your life who can collectively meet them, takes work but is far more achievable.[15] This applies not only to DEI, but to our lives more broadly. Use this exercise when you're looking to brainstorm ways to expand your support network.

LEARNING GOALS

- Identify and define the needs that are most important to you.
- Identify your existing support network of people who can help meet your needs.
- Make plans to increase your support network to help meet unmet needs.

UNDERSTAND YOURSELF

EXPAND YOUR CAPACITY

RELY ON OTHERS

FIND YOUR PLACE

DIAGNOSE INEQUITY

CHAMPION INCLUSION

ADDRESS CONFLICT AND HARM

ORGANIZE A MOVEMENT

REIMAGINE SYSTEMS

ACHIEVE DEI

INSTRUCTIONS

Learn about what needs are, and examples of different types of needs. Fill out the chart under My Needs and Anchors with your most important needs, what they mean to you, and sources in your life that help you meet each need. Then, if you have one or more anchors who you primarily trust, rely on, and feel close to who can meet that need, name them in the final column. If not, leave the final column blank. Then, answer the reflection questions.

What Are Needs?

Needs are things required for people to live a full life. While all people share physical needs like food, water, clothing, and shelter, each person has unique needs that are most important to them and that make them feel like something important in their life is missing if they are not met. Examples of these needs include companionship, love, exercise, productivity, adventure, novelty, accountability, patience, and stability.[16] Each person has a different set of needs, and even two people with the same needs might define them in different ways.

1. What seven needs are most important to you outside of physical/survival needs?

1.	
2.	
3.	
4.	
5.	
6.	
7.	

2. How did you come to this list of seven? How did you feel while choosing them?

_____

_____

_____

_____

3. Thinking about this list of needs, how do you know when you *don't* have these needs met? How do you feel when this is the case?

_____

_____

_____

_____

4. Thinking about this list of needs, how do you know when you *do* have these needs met? How do you feel when this is the case?

_____

_____

_____

5. Fill out the following chart with the needs you chose. For each, define what the need means to you. Then, name some of the sources in your life that help you meet that need. You can name individual people, organizations, activities, or anything else. Finally, if among those sources you listed something or someone that you especially and regularly trust and rely on to meet that need, list them as an anchor in the final column. If not, leave the final column blank. Then, answer the reflection questions.

My Needs and Anchors

NEED	DEFINITION	I MEET MY NEED THROUGH	ANCHOR(S)
Learning	Regular experiences that increase my skills and knowledge in domains I care about	▪ Online newsletters ▪ E-learning courses ▪ My manager ▪ My colleague Andy	My colleague Andy, who always shares exciting research with me whenever he comes across it

CONTINUED ▶

UNDERSTAND YOURSELF

EXPAND YOUR CAPACITY

RELY ON OTHERS

FIND YOUR PLACE

DIAGNOSE INEQUITY

CHAMPION INCLUSION

ADDRESS CONFLICT AND HARM

ORGANIZE A MOVEMENT

REIMAGINE SYSTEMS

ACHIEVE DEI

NEED	DEFINITION	I MEET MY NEED THROUGH	ANCHOR(S)

REFLECTION QUESTIONS

1. How was the process of defining your needs for you? Which was the hardest to define?

_____

_____

_____

_____

2. Which of your needs do you have the *fewest* ways to meet? Why might that be?

_____

_____

_____

3. Which of your needs do you have the *most* ways to meet? Why might that be?

_____

_____

_____

4. Which of your needs don't yet have anchors, and why?

_____

_____

_____

_____

UNDERSTAND YOURSELF

EXPAND YOUR CAPACITY

RELY ON OTHERS

FIND YOUR PLACE

DIAGNOSE INEQUITY

CHAMPION INCLUSION

ADDRESS CONFLICT AND HARM

ORGANIZE A MOVEMENT

REIMAGINE SYSTEMS

ACHIEVE DEI

5. Think of how you found ways to meet your needs throughout your life. What strategies did you use?

_____

_____

_____

_____

6. How might you use similar strategies to meet needs that you aren't currently meeting, or find anchors for needs without them?

_____

_____

_____

_____

7. How might you strengthen or sustain the needs that are currently being met?

_____

_____

_____

_____

8. Overall, how has your perspective regarding your own needs and how you're meeting them changed after this exercise, if at all?

_____

_____

_____

_____

NOTES

15. Scott, Brianna, and Mallika Seshadri. "Consider This: They Say You Can't Choose Your Family, but Some People Do." All Things Considered, January 2, 2023. https://www.npr.org/2023/01/02/1146588160/consider-this-they-say-you-cant-choose-your-family-but-some-people-do.

16. Spacey, John. "90 Examples of Human Needs." Simplicable, May 9, 2022. https://simplicable.com/society/human-needs.

" ANCHORS CAN HELP
MEET OUR DEEPEST
AND MOST IMPORTANT NEEDS
SO THAT WE FEEL STEADY
AND CENTERED WHEN DOING
DEI WORK.

10

Ask for Help

Asking for help is an easy skill to talk about, and a deceptively challenging skill to use. The biggest challenge isn't in its difficulty, but in the self-imposed barriers many practitioners put up to even admitting they need help, let alone making an attempt to ask for it. An all-too-common mindset is assuming that DEI work can be done alone up until the point where the challenges are too big to handle, and only then should a practitioner seek assistance. The problem with this mindset is that in many cases, by the time you recognize you're in over your head, the difficulties you're facing are simply too large to resolve easily. It's one thing to refuel a car with a quarter or half-full tank remaining. It's another to realize you need to refuel when your car's engine shuts off and you have to push it along the side of the road to make it to the next station.

Knowing how to ask for help, especially as a preventative measure and not as a desperate one, allows us to be more stable and grounded within what can often be an unpredictable line of work. It both unlocks solutions and approaches that we ourselves wouldn't know if we worked on our own, and protects us from burning ourselves out.

LEARNING GOALS

- Learn about the building blocks of an effective request for help.
- Create your own request for help, and practice actually making it.
- Brainstorm contextual factors that make it easier or harder to ask for help.

INSTRUCTIONS

Read the example of an effective request for help, and follow the prompts to fill out the blank chart with a request for help you might make in your own organization. Afterwards, answer the reflection questions.

Effective Requests for Help

An effective request for help encapsulates the "five W's"—who, what, where, when, and why—and is tailored for a specific "how." An example chart is provided.

WHO	WHAT	WHERE	WHEN	WHY	HOW
My manager Jessica	Setting aside a protected time for additional comments	The all-team meeting	Next week	One colleague makes it difficult to get a word in edgewise; other colleagues' thoughts go unheard; my manager can set meeting agendas.	At the end of our usual 1:1 meeting and with follow-up resources

FULLY ASSEMBLED REQUEST
Jessica, could I ask you for your help in adding a short 5-minute item to the agenda for the next meeting, for people to share additional comments? Our meetings move quickly and I've noticed that it can be difficult to hear thoughts from our full team, especially if one or two people dominate the airtime. I think this small change will make a difference and improve the quality of our meetings. Thanks for considering it! I'd also be happy to send some research and resources I found related to this if that interests you.

1. What might you ask for help with as a DEI practitioner or inclusive leader? Some ideas might include "sharing information about a department in the organization," "help facilitating a workshop," "space to share emotions or vent," or "thought partnership." Use the lines here to list your own ideas.

1.	2.
3.	4.
5.	6.
7.	8.
9.	10.

2. Out of these, pick one issue or topic that you are willing to ask an actual person for help with as part of this exercise, and enter it below.

_____

_____

_____

_____

3. Next, answer the prompts to fill in the table with your own effective request for help.

WHO	WHAT	WHERE	WHEN	WHY	HOW
Who is your request for?	What is it you want them to do to help you?	Where do you want them to help?	When do you want them to help?	Why is their help required, and why did you ask them specifically for help?	How will you make the request effectively?

FULLY ASSEMBLED REQUEST

4. What do you think might be challenging about making the request you developed?

_____

_____

_____

_____

UNDERSTAND YOURSELF

EXPAND YOUR CAPACITY

RELY ON OTHERS

FIND YOUR PLACE

DIAGNOSE INEQUITY

CHAMPION INCLUSION

ADDRESS CONFLICT AND HARM

ORGANIZE A MOVEMENT

REIMAGINE SYSTEMS

ACHIEVE DEI

5. What do you think would be the outcome of making that request to the person(s) you chose? Do you feel confident that you would receive the help you asked for? Why or why not?

_____

_____

_____

_____

6. How will you follow up if they agree to your request? Lay out some next steps.

_____

_____

_____

_____

7. How will you follow up if they cannot fulfill your request? Lay out some next steps.

_____

_____

_____

_____

8. Finally, try reaching out to ask for help in the way you outlined, utilizing your fully assembled request for help with who, what, where, when, why, and how. You may feel nervous or slightly uncomfortable, especially if you don't ask for help often—these are normal things to feel and will become easier to manage with practice. Afterwards, answer the reflection questions.

REFLECTION QUESTIONS

1. How did the conversation go? To what extent were the five W's (and one H) helpful in making your request?

_____

_____

_____

_____

2. What was the hardest part about asking for help? Why do you think that was the case?

_____

_____

_____

_____

This exercise focuses on your personal abilities to ask for help. However, oftentimes factors beyond our direct control, like the mood of the person we're asking, the timing of our request, or the broader political climate, might make it easier or harder to have our request met.

3. Thinking about your request, what factors might have made it *easier* for you to ask for help, or easier for someone to accept your request?

_____

_____

_____

4. Thinking about your request, what factors might have made it *harder* for you to ask for help, or harder for them to accept your request?

_____

_____

_____

_____

5. In hindsight, if you could have changed anything about your request for help, what would you have changed and why?

_____

_____

_____

_____

NOTE

17. Huang, Karen, Michael Yeomans, Alison Wood Brooks, Julia Minson, and Francesca Gino. "It doesn't hurt to ask: Question-asking increases liking." *Journal of Personality and Social Psychology* 113, no. 3 (2017): 430. https://doi.org/10.1037/pspi0000097.

UNDERSTAND YOURSELF

EXPAND YOUR CAPACITY

RELY ON OTHERS

FIND YOUR PLACE

DIAGNOSE INEQUITY

CHAMPION INCLUSION

ADDRESS CONFLICT AND HARM

ORGANIZE A MOVEMENT

REIMAGINE SYSTEMS

ACHIEVE DEI

11

Set Boundaries

The opposite skill to asking for help is being able to give the humble "no," and otherwise set and maintain proactive boundaries related to our time, energy, comfort, and commitment. This is critical for practitioners, especially because many of us are so empathetic, passionate, and helpful that, without boundaries, what might start out looking like generosity might end up becoming over-extension and subsequently burnout.[18]

Many practitioners find out the hard way that when they're unable to say no, they can quickly end up with too many responsibilities and tasks to do any of them effectively, and suffer hits to their physical and mental health, as well as their efficacy and impact, as a result. Personal and professional boundaries may feel unintuitive and even "cruel" to those who are unused to them, but they are in fact one of the kindest things we can do for ourselves and others. Good boundaries ensure that we can reliably and sustainably keep the promises and commitments we make.

PRACTITIONER'S TIP

Giving a no in the heat of the moment to protect your boundaries is just plain hard, especially when there's external pressure to say yes. Our fight-flight-freeze-fawn instinct flares up. We may sweat, fidget, and feel anxious. That's why one of the most useful tools to get better at protecting these boundaries is setting them proactively, during a neutral and low-stress occasion. Doing so not only makes it easier to say no when asked to do something that oversteps our boundaries, but also dramatically lessens the likelihood that we'll be asked to do so in the first place. Use this exercise whenever you're looking for structured support for ideating about and setting new boundaries.

LEARNING GOALS

- List personal examples of the six kinds of boundaries in your own life.
- Pick a boundary you want to set, and make a plan for how you'll set it.
- Discover personal insight into what kinds of boundaries feel hardest to set in DEI work.

INSTRUCTIONS

Read the following passage, Effective Boundaries. Then, review the six types of effective boundaries on the chart, and fill in the rest of the chart with examples of your own boundaries from each type. Work through the rest of the exercise questions, and finally, answer the reflection questions.

Effective Boundaries

An effective interpersonal boundary has two major components: a clearly communicated limit placed by you between yourself and others, and a personal commitment from you to enforce that limit. If the limit isn't clearly set, or if your enforcement of it isn't consistent, that boundary will be easily crossed or violated by yourself or others. On the chart, each of the six types of boundaries is defined and an example is given. For each, list an example that you could see yourself setting.

BOUNDARY	DEFINITION	EXAMPLE	YOUR EXAMPLE
Time	How much time you want to spend with somebody or doing something	Ending a meeting at a specific time so you can make it to an important event	
Material	How much of a resource (often, money) you want to spend or give	Setting a funding limit for an event to ensure that the other events that quarter are funded too	
Physical	Related to your body or personal space	Asking your colleagues to refrain from touching your hair or clothing	
Information	How much information you want to share, related to privacy	After colleagues share "fun facts" about their marital status, sharing a different kind of fun fact	
Emotional	How much emotional labor or support you want to spend or give	Respectfully declining a colleague's request for emotional support at the end of the day	
Intellectual	Related to your ideas, thoughts, and communication	Leaving a conversation where you're not feeling respected or listened to	

1. In your own life, what *types* of boundaries feel hardest to set, and why?

_____

_____

_____

_____

2. Setting boundaries with someone who is your peer or who has less power than you do can feel very different from doing so with someone who has more power than you. What unique challenges might occur when you try to do the latter?

_____

_____

_____

_____

3. What would you say are the *most important* boundaries you might set as a DEI practitioner or inclusive leader? Why are they important?

_____

_____

_____

_____

4. Out of these, pick one boundary that you are willing to set with an actual person as part of this exercise, and enter it below.

_____

_____

_____

_____

UNDERSTAND YOURSELF

EXPAND YOUR CAPACITY

RELY ON OTHERS

FIND YOUR PLACE

DIAGNOSE INEQUITY

CHAMPION INCLUSION

ADDRESS CONFLICT AND HARM

ORGANIZE A MOVEMENT

REIMAGINE SYSTEMS

ACHIEVE DEI

5. Consider the following framework, prompts, and example answers for formulating a boundary.

WHO	WHAT	WHERE	WHEN	WHY	HOW
Who will you set the boundary with? *My coworker Sam*	What boundary will you set? *Hard time limits on meetings*	Where does this boundary apply? *Our 1:1 meetings*	When does this boundary apply? *Every meeting*	Why does this boundary need to be set? (This answer does not need to go into your request itself.) *Sam will drive every conversation for hours unless told not to from the start.*	How will you make the request effectively? *In email before our next 1:1, and verbally at the start of it*

FULLY ASSEMBLED REQUEST
Hi Sam, it's good to see you today! Before we get started, I want to request that we stay on track to finish up the agenda we talked about by the end of the hour. Your insights are extremely valuable, and I know also that some of our meetings have run quite long—which can make it hard for me to prioritize my other work. I'd like us to keep an eye on the time and set the expectation that I sign off at the top of the hour. Could you help me with that?

6. Next, answer the prompts to fill in the table with your own effective request for help.

WHO	WHAT	WHERE	WHEN	WHY	HOW
Who is your request for?	What is it you want them to do to help you?	Where do you want them to help?	When do you want them to help?	Why is their help required, and why did you ask them specifically for help?	How will you make the request effectively?

FULLY ASSEMBLED REQUEST

7. What do you think would be the outcome of making that request to the person(s) you chose? Do you feel confident that you would receive the help you asked for? Why or why not?

_____

_____

_____

_____

8. Finally, try setting the boundary in the way you outlined, utilizing your fully assembled request with who, what, where, when, why, and how. You may feel nervous or slightly uncomfortable, especially if you don't set boundaries often—these are normal things to feel and will become easier to manage with practice.

REFLECTION QUESTIONS

1. How did the conversation go? To what extent were the five W's (and one H) helpful in making your request?

_____

_____

_____

_____

2. What was the hardest part about setting a boundary? Why do you think that was the case?

_____

_____

_____

_____

3. In hindsight, if you could have changed anything about your boundary-setting effort, what would you have changed and why?

_____

_____

_____

_____

UNDERSTAND YOURSELF

EXPAND YOUR CAPACITY

RELY ON OTHERS

FIND YOUR PLACE

DIAGNOSE INEQUITY

CHAMPION INCLUSION

ADDRESS CONFLICT AND HARM

ORGANIZE A MOVEMENT

REIMAGINE SYSTEMS

ACHIEVE DEI

4. In the future, how might you get more experience and comfort with setting boundaries, especially those that are harder for you?

_____

_____

_____

_____

5. What kinds of boundaries might be most challenging *within DEI work* to set and maintain for practitioners or inclusive leaders? Brainstorm a list.

1.	2.
3.	4.
5.	6.
7.	8.

6. If you were to give tips on setting these boundaries effectively to another person, what would you say?

_____

_____

_____

_____

_____

_____

_____

_____

_____

NOTE

18. Grant, Adam, and Reb Rebele. "Beat Generosity Burnout." Harvard Business Review, January 23, 2017. https://hbr.org/2017/01/beat-generosity-burnout.

" AN EFFECTIVE
INTERPERSONAL BOUNDARY
HAS TWO MAJOR COMPONENTS:
A CLEARLY COMMUNICATED
LIMIT PLACED BY YOU BETWEEN
YOURSELF AND OTHERS,
AND A PERSONAL COMMITMENT
FROM YOU TO ENFORCE
THAT LIMIT.

12

Accept Accountability

Relying on others allows us to better achieve our own goals, as well as those goals that can't just be accomplished on our own. One particularly valuable form of interpersonal reliance is shared accountability: relationships involving mutual social commitments to hold each other responsible, regularly check in, and exchange motivation and coaching to achieve goals that we choose for ourselves. Shared accountability is most useful for complex, multistep challenges that are hard or impossible to solve in one sitting—like DEI work, for example.

And creating it requires every skill in this section, from identifying your anchors to asking for help to setting boundaries.

Building shared accountability for DEI work is a practice that relies on strong awareness of our DEI goals, a solid understanding of our colleagues and the people around us, and the skills to request as well as provide help. This skill is challenging to put into practice, but it's more than made up for by the reward of having a trusted partner alongside you as you do the work.[19]

PRACTITIONER'S TIP

The people most suited for shared accountability will likely change depending on our goals. For example, creating a relationship of shared accountability for speaking up during a meeting if someone makes a harmful comment can only happen effectively with someone else present at that meeting. Shared accountability for achieving a set amount of progress on a project is more effective with someone working on a similar kind of project. Use this exercise when you're looking to brainstorm how, and with whom, you want to create shared accountability.

LEARNING GOALS

- Understand the qualities and factors that make people good fits for shared accountability.
- List your short-term DEI goals, and brainstorm a list of people who might be good fits for shared accountability.
- Create and deliver a request for shared accountability to at least one person.

UNDERSTAND YOURSELF

EXPAND YOUR CAPACITY

RELY ON OTHERS

FIND YOUR PLACE

DIAGNOSE INEQUITY

CHAMPION INCLUSION

ADDRESS CONFLICT AND HARM

ORGANIZE A MOVEMENT

REIMAGINE SYSTEMS

ACHIEVE DEI

INSTRUCTIONS

Learn about shared accountability. Then, answer the exercise questions to list your short-term DEI goals, and follow the prompts to fill out the chart with people who might be good fits for shared accountability. Afterwards, answer the reflection questions.

Who to Seek Out for Shared Accountability

When it comes to accountability, there are a number of traits that stand out as obvious pluses: discipline, patience, and empathy, for example. We want those we seek accountability from to keep us on task, challenge us, and yet also be understanding and empathetic rather than inflexible drill sergeants. That said, these skills can be learned. The surprising reality is that accountability is more about the fit between the person we ask, the goal we want to achieve, and the context we want to achieve it in than individual skill alone.

If we ask someone who we have a personal relationship to, who might have similar goals, and who is operating in a similar context, that relationship might end up as a more powerful source of shared accountability compared to one with someone who we don't know, has different goals, or is working in a very different context regardless of people's individual traits or skills.

It begins with having a specific goal or goals: the more we define what we're trying to achieve, the more likely we are to be able to tailor our outreach to people best suited to help.

1. With what concrete and specific DEI goals might you benefit from shared accountability in the next few weeks and months? List four goals under the two examples.

1. Emotional support dealing with the aftermath of a mass layoff
2. Speaking up when witnessing instances of bias or subtle acts of exclusion
3.
4.
5.
6.

2. For each goal, answer the prompts to fill out the chart. A sample chart is provided.

GOAL What are you trying to achieve?	PROXIMAL PEOPLE Who do you interact with regularly who might help?	GOAL ALIGNMENT Who might share the same goal?	SKILL FIT ... and have patience/discipline/empathy?
Emotional support dealing with the aftermath of a mass layoff	■ Project partner Tim ■ Manager Monique ■ Colleague Sam ■ Teammate Ryan	■ Project partner Tim ■ Teammate Ryan	■ Teammate Ryan
Speaking up when witnessing bias or subtle acts of exclusion	■ Project partner Tim ■ Teammate Ryan ■ Teammate Dinah ■ Teammate Andrea	■ Teammate Dinah ■ Teammate Andrea	■ Teammate Dinah ■ Teammate Andrea

GOAL What are you trying to achieve?	PROXIMAL PEOPLE Who do you interact with regularly who might help?	GOAL ALIGNMENT Who might share the same goal?	SKILL FIT ... and have patience/discipline/empathy?

3. Out of these, pick one goal you are willing to seek out shared accountability for as part of this exercise, and enter it below.

_____

_____

_____

_____

UNDERSTAND YOURSELF

EXPAND YOUR CAPACITY

RELY ON OTHERS

FIND YOUR PLACE

DIAGNOSE INEQUITY

CHAMPION INCLUSION

ADDRESS CONFLICT AND HARM

ORGANIZE A MOVEMENT

REIMAGINE SYSTEMS

ACHIEVE DEI

4. Then, use the modified framework and the following prompts to formulate how you will reach out to request shared accountability. A sample chart is provided.

WHO	WHAT	WHERE/WHEN	ACTION	HOW
Who will you request accountability from? *My teammate Dinah*	What goal do you want to achieve? *Speaking up as upstanders after biased comments*	Where and when should accountability take place? *Our team meetings*	What action will you take together to achieve the shared goal? *When we witness bias, we'll confirm it in a private message to each other and take turns speaking up*	How will you make the request effectively? *I'll send a request to meet about it*

FULLY ASSEMBLED REQUEST
Hi Dinah, thanks for agreeing to meet! I reached out because I remember the conversation we had a few weeks ago about speaking up more when we encounter biased comments during our meetings and I have an idea. Would you be interested in working with me to respond to biased comments together during meetings, and provide mutual accountability? I was thinking that if we're both present, we can send a quick DM to each other to confirm that the comment was biased, then take turns speaking up to challenge it. We could check in after meetings also to hold each other accountable. What do you think?

WHO	WHAT	WHERE/WHEN	ACTION	HOW
Who will you request accountability from?	What goal do you want to achieve?	Where and when should accountability take place?	What action will you take together to achieve the shared goal?	How will you make the request effectively?

FULLY ASSEMBLED REQUEST

5. What do you think would be the outcome of making that request to the person(s) you chose? Do you feel confident that you would receive the accountability you asked for? Why or why not?

_____

_____

_____

_____

6. Finally, try reaching out for shared accountability in the way you outlined, utilizing your fully assembled request with who, what, where/when, the action you want to take, and how. You may feel nervous or slightly uncomfortable, especially if you don't request mutual accountability often—these are normal things to feel and will become easier to manage with practice.

REFLECTION QUESTIONS

1. How did the conversation go? To what extent was your outline helpful in making your request?

_____

_____

_____

_____

2. What was the hardest part about requesting shared accountability? Why do you think that was the case?

_____

_____

_____

_____

3. In hindsight, if you could have changed anything about your accountability request, what would you have changed and why?

4. Now that you've done so once, what other goals—DEI-related or not—can you imagine potentially seeking out shared accountability to achieve?

5. Those best suited to providing shared accountability are able to embody discipline, patience, and empathy. How might you intentionally take action to hone these skills in your own practice moving forward, so that you may provide effective accountability for others?

6. If more people in your organization sought out and utilized shared accountability, what might some of the benefits be?

NOTE

19. Barzacchini, Mike. "How to Be an Accountability Partner—#MTtalk Roundup." MindTools, March 29, 2022. https://www.mindtools.com/blog/how-to-be-an-accountability-partner-mttalk-roundup/.

" ACCOUNTABILITY IS MORE ABOUT THE FIT BETWEEN THE PERSON WE ASK, THE GOAL WE WANT TO ACHIEVE, AND THE CONTEXT WE WANT TO ACHIEVE IT IN THAN INDIVIDUAL SKILL ALONE.

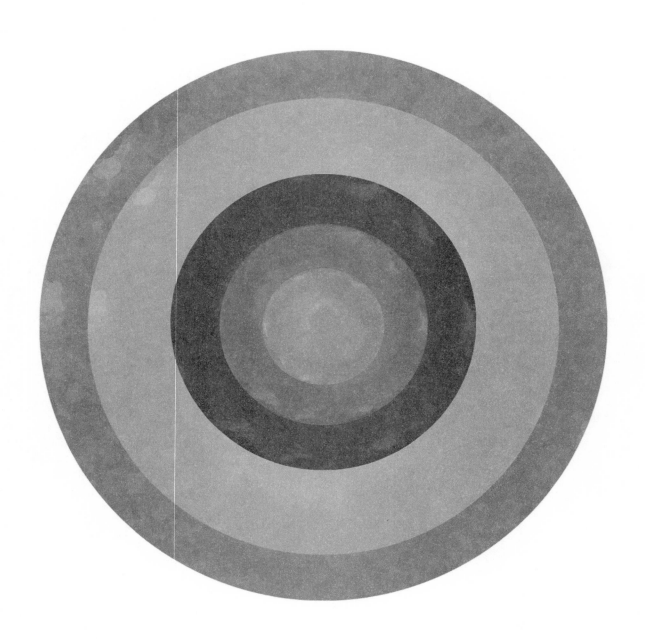

Hone Your Skills

FIND YOUR PLACE

DEI practitioners often use the term *positionality* to describe how our unique combinations of identities affect our experiences in society.[20] We already explored a key dimension of positionality earlier, when we explored the role of social identity in our expertise and experiences, but there's more to learn beyond just this. Understanding how our roles within the workplaces, organizations, and communities we occupy affect our experiences allows us to flesh out our self-awareness even further and begin applying this understanding in our actions.

> ❝ UNDERSTANDING OUR PLACE IN THE ORGANIZATION AND WITHIN MOVEMENTS ALLOWS US TO SITUATE OURSELVES IN THE BIGGER PICTURE OF DEI WORK.

While identity is important, it's also not everything on its own. A CEO lacking in privilege due to being from multiple marginalized groups still has enormous privilege and power from being a CEO. A disabled White woman able to skillfully navigate identity and deploy power as a middle manager is very different from the same person without those skills. A Black, gay man able to maximize his role in a social movement to create change is very different from the same person without that ability. Overlooking our

formal authority, access to power, and contextual power within movements means ignoring the dynamism of positionality in practice.

It can result in a false sense of security and a lack of accountability if we allow ourselves to assume that we can never be part of the problem. It can result in diminished efficacy if we don't think carefully about how the advocacy and leadership we engage in align with our organization and movement roles. Understanding our place in the organization and within movements, and how our full positionality affects our experiences, allows us to situate ourselves in the bigger picture of DEI work. That's positionality at its most useful: not a static designation of privilege or marginalization, but a living, breathing reflection of ourselves in all our complexity.

---

20. WI+RE Creative Design Team. "Positionality & Research: How Our Identities Shape Inquiry." YouTube, March 16, 2021. https://www.youtube.com/watch?v=fTHFud7fr8c.

13

Name What You Steward

Everyone, in every organization and in every community, is responsible for something. For some, it can be as formal and large as the responsibility to lead an entire company. For others, it can be as informal and simple as the shared responsibility to keep a space clean. While responsibility might feel mundane to name, it's actually quite powerful—responsibility can be a source of pride, purpose, personal power, and influence. By naming both the obvious and less obvious responsibilities we have, as well as the related systems, processes, policies, practices, and so on that we steward, we can start to understand our role in our larger environments.

This isn't just an intellectual exercise. Knowing how we fit in to the larger whole of our organizations and communities directly spells out for us our ideal avenues to create change. Our responsibilities directly translate to our *power*, and naming these responsibilities out loud can help us start strategizing where we might focus our change efforts on first.

PRACTITIONER'S TIP

It can be challenging for people not in formal leadership positions to feel a clear sense of stewardship in their own roles. In my own work, I've spoken many times with professionals who were taking on an enormous amount of DEI-related responsibility and yet were having difficulty owning or articulating it. Taking another angle, we can outline responsibility by instead asking, "What things would fall apart if you were no longer there?" For many, this question helps them realize just how valuable their work is and how much influence they have as a result. Use this exercise whenever you're looking to gain a better perspective on the work you're taking on or strategize about how you might make the most impact.

LEARNING GOALS

- Name and categorize your formal and informal responsibilities.
- Connect your responsibilities to the systems, processes, policies, and practices under your stewardship.
- Clearly articulate avenues to initiate change using your responsibilities as a guide.

UNDERSTAND YOURSELF

EXPAND YOUR CAPACITY

RELY ON OTHERS

FIND YOUR PLACE

DIAGNOSE INEQUITY

CHAMPION INCLUSION

ADDRESS CONFLICT AND HARM

ORGANIZE A MOVEMENT

REIMAGINE SYSTEMS

ACHIEVE DEI

INSTRUCTIONS

Answer exercise questions 1–3 to outline your own responsibilities and what they indicate about your stewardship. Then, read the chart to learn about the four types of responsibilities, and answer the rest of the questions with examples from your own organization or community. Afterwards, answer the reflection questions.

1. When you think of your formal responsibilities within your organization or community, what are the first three or four things that come to mind?

_____

_____

_____

_____

2. If you were to leave the organization or community tomorrow, what would change most dramatically from your sudden absence? Why?

_____

_____

_____

3. What do your answers to questions 1 and 2 tell you about what policies, processes, practices, and people at your organization or community depend on you?

_____

_____

_____

_____

We can think of responsibilities within organizations as falling under four different types.

TYPE	DEFINITION	EXAMPLE
Task responsibility	The responsibility to execute a defined task	■ Talk to customers ■ Analyze data ■ Schedule meetings ■ Clean up a shared space
Outcome responsibility	The responsibility to ensure a specific end result or outcome	■ Making sure customers feel listened to ■ Making sure clear findings from data get shared ■ Making sure meetings are run effectively ■ Making sure the shared space stays clean
Stewardship responsibility	The responsibility to define, represent, or safeguard important systems, processes, or ideals, often from the top down	■ Owning the anonymous feedback process ■ Using data at every level to inform decisions ■ Modeling respect for each other's time in meetings ■ Distributing responsibility for cleaning the shared space fairly
Shared responsibility	The collective responsibility to maintain important systems, processes, or ideals, often from the bottom up	■ Maintaining healthy customer relationships ■ Sustaining a data-driven culture ■ Upholding a commitment to make all interactions respectful ■ Maintaining a culture of shared responsibility for shared space

4. Task responsibilities are about executing defined tasks. What task responsibilities do you have in your organization or community?

_____

_____

_____

_____

5. Outcome responsibilities are about ensuring specific end results or outcomes. What outcome responsibilities do you have in your organization or community?

_____

_____

_____

_____

UNDERSTAND YOURSELF

EXPAND YOUR CAPACITY

RELY ON OTHERS

FIND YOUR PLACE

DIAGNOSE INEQUITY

CHAMPION INCLUSION

ADDRESS CONFLICT AND HARM

ORGANIZE A MOVEMENT

REIMAGINE SYSTEMS

ACHIEVE DEI

6. Stewardship responsibilities are about defining, representing, or safeguarding important systems, processes, or ideals, often from the top down. What stewardship responsibilities do you have in your organization or community?

_____

_____

_____

_____

7. Shared responsibilities are about collectively maintaining important systems, processes, or ideals, often from the bottom up. What shared responsibilities do you have in your organization or community?

_____

_____

_____

_____

REFLECTION QUESTIONS

1. Review how your responsibilities are distributed across task, outcome, stewardship, and shared responsibilities. Which kinds carry the most vs. the least responsibility?

_____

_____

_____

_____

2. While task and outcome responsibilities are likely to be included in our job descriptions, stewardship and shared responsibilities are often not. How might you engage in your stewardship and shared responsibilities more intentionally going forward?

_____

_____

_____

_____

3. Your existing responsibilities can inform your initial advocacy or change-making strategy within DEI work. Given your distribution of responsibilities, where do you see the potential to make the most DEI-related impact, and what might those efforts look like?

_____

_____

_____

_____

14

Determine Your Power

Many of us think about power solely as formal authority or responsibility (essentially, what a manager or executive has), and if we don't possess this power, we believe we must not possess power at all. But this viewpoint is too narrow. Power is the ability to influence an outcome, and under this definition *everyone* has access to some of it.

Scholars of power typically think of power as having at least *six* different types, many of them informal.[21] Power isn't just formal authority, but also the ability to give rewards or threaten punishment, the possession of important information or expertise, and access to valuable connections or interpersonal charisma. Understanding how to identify your access to these other types of power is like trading in a screwdriver for a Swiss Army knife: by expanding the tools at your disposal, it dramatically increases your ability to create the outcomes you want.

PRACTITIONER'S TIP

Many DEI practitioners and advocates are leery about leveraging power in their own advocacy, concerned that even engaging with power opens up the possibility that they will abuse it. This is an understandable fear! We've all seen or heard examples of people who gained power, only to misuse it. But power is already around us, embedded in the systems we engage with every day. Whether or not we choose to exercise our own power, power is always being exercised on and around us. If we can't divest immediately and entirely from these power dynamics, then it behooves us to build an understanding of how they function, and leverage them toward our goals of diversity, equity, and inclusion. Use this exercise when you're looking for a reminder of the power you have access to and encouragement to utilize it.

LEARNING GOALS

- Learn about the six different types of power, and categorize examples from your own context under them.
- Explore different avenues to achieving your DEI goals and how they relate to each type of power.
- Identify the types of power you have more or less of, and discuss the implications.

UNDERSTAND YOURSELF

EXPAND YOUR CAPACITY

RELY ON OTHERS

FIND YOUR PLACE

DIAGNOSE INEQUITY

CHAMPION INCLUSION

ADDRESS CONFLICT AND HARM

ORGANIZE A MOVEMENT

REIMAGINE SYSTEMS

ACHIEVE DEI

INSTRUCTIONS

The following chart lists different types of power—formal, reward, coercive, expert, information, and referent—alongside their definitions and examples of their use. Fill out the chart with examples of how you would use your access to power in these categories—some may be easier to brainstorm than others—then answer the exercise questions.

POWER	DEFINITION	EXAMPLE OF ITS USE	YOUR EXAMPLE
Formal	The right or authority to request behavior from another	"I need you to complete this task by the end of the week."	
Reward	The ability to promise (monetary or nonmonetary) compensation to influence behavior	"If you help me with this task, I'll put in a good word for you with this person you've wanted to speak to."	
Coercive	The ability to threaten punishment to influence behavior	"If you don't complete this task, it'll go into your performance evaluation."	
Expert	The ability to influence behavior by being seen as possessing greater expertise	"I highly recommend you focus on these tasks if you want to achieve that outcome."	
Information	The ability to influence behavior by possessing greater information	"I just heard from a trustworthy source that this particular task is especially valuable to complete right now."	
Referent	The ability to build rapport and influence behavior through charisma	"It'd mean a lot to me if you helped me complete this task."	

1. For the kind of power you have the *least* of, what limitations does that put on your advocacy? These limitations can help you strategize on what allies and coalitions to engage with.

_____

_____

_____

_____

2. For the kind of power you have the *most* of, what opportunities does that give your advocacy? These opportunities can help you strategize on what allies and coalitions to engage with.

_____

_____

_____

_____

3. Imagine a future where you're able to achieve your DEI goals primarily through *formal power*. What might that future look like? What would it take for you to reach that future?

_____

_____

_____

_____

4. Imagine a future where you're able to achieve your DEI goals primarily through *reward power*. What might that future look like? What would it take for you to reach that future?

_____

_____

_____

_____

UNDERSTAND YOURSELF

EXPAND YOUR CAPACITY

RELY ON OTHERS

FIND YOUR PLACE

DIAGNOSE INEQUITY

CHAMPION INCLUSION

ADDRESS CONFLICT AND HARM

ORGANIZE A MOVEMENT

REIMAGINE SYSTEMS

ACHIEVE DEI

5. Imagine a future where you can to achieve your DEI goals primarily through *coercive power*. What might that future look like? What would it take for you to reach that future?

_____

_____

_____

_____

6. Imagine a future where you're able to achieve your DEI goals primarily through *expert power*. What might that future look like? What would it take for you to reach that future?

_____

_____

_____

_____

7. Imagine a future where you're able to achieve your DEI goals primarily through *information power*. What might that future look like? What would it take for you to reach that future?

_____

_____

_____

_____

8. Imagine a future where you're able to achieve your DEI goals primarily through *referent power*. What might that future look like? What would it take for you to reach that future?

_____

_____

_____

_____

NOTE

21. MindTools Content Team. "French and Raven's Five Forms of Power." MindTools, June 22, 2009. https://www.mindtools.com/abwzix3/french-and-ravens-five-forms-of-power.

" POWER IS ALREADY AROUND US, EMBEDDED IN THE SYSTEMS WE ENGAGE WITH EVERY DAY. WHETHER OR NOT WE CHOOSE TO EXERCISE OUR OWN POWER, POWER IS ALWAYS BEING EXERCISED ON AND AROUND US.

15

Recognize Opportunity

Our identities affect our life experiences and our expertise, as we explored earlier. But while our identities remain more or less constant across different environments, the opportunities they grant us do not. In some settings, when most of our identities match those of the people around us, we blend in. Our expertise is likely to be shared by others, and our identities themselves might not even stand out to us unless otherwise brought to our attention. In other settings, one or more of our identities stands out as different. We may be the only one in the room with a particular identity, and as a result, one of few people with the expertise we have. While our identities haven't changed, the opportunity we have to leverage them effectively certainly has.

Recognizing these opportunities requires moving one step beyond awareness of identity into awareness of *context* and how our identities interact with it. If we can recognize when we're well set up to make change, we can prepare ourselves to act and take effective action.

> **PRACTITIONER'S TIP**
>
> Recognizing an opportunity to take effective action does not mean you always have to act! Be mindful of your personal capacity and the risks and benefits of taking action. The goal of building this skill is not to be constantly jumping to act on your expertise, but instead to be able to recognize the many situations you might act in, picking your battles and using your time, energy, and power wisely. Use this exercise to refresh your skills at recognizing contextual opportunity and to plan out how you might leverage your identities and expertise to act in the moment.

LEARNING GOALS

- Name environments in which you feel like part of the majority vs. part of the minority, and contextualize your identity-related expertise within both.
- Strategize about how you might leverage your identity expertise to take action on DEI within different environments.

UNDERSTAND YOURSELF

EXPAND YOUR CAPACITY

RELY ON OTHERS

FIND YOUR PLACE

DIAGNOSE INEQUITY

CHAMPION INCLUSION

ADDRESS CONFLICT AND HARM

ORGANIZE A MOVEMENT

REIMAGINE SYSTEMS

ACHIEVE DEI

INSTRUCTIONS

Answer the exercise questions to name environments or contexts in which you are part of the majority vs. part of the minority, then select two from each. Follow the prompts to fill out the chart with examples of how you might leverage those identities to take action or advocate for DEI. Afterwards, answer the reflection questions.

1. List several environments or contexts in which you feel like you belong to the *majority group* on the basis of one or more identities that are important to you.

1.	4.
2.	5.
3.	6.

2. List several environments or contexts in which you feel like you belong to the *minority group*, especially if you're the only person of a certain identity, on the basis of one or more identities that are important to you.

1.	4.
2.	5.
3.	6.

3. Pick two environments from each list, and follow the prompts to fill out the chart on the opposite page. Sample environments and answers are included.

REFLECTION QUESTIONS

1. What do you feel is the biggest difference between opportunities related to your majority identity expertise vs. opportunities related to your minority identity expertise?

_____

_____

_____

_____

CONTEXT	MAJORITY/ MINORITY IDENTITY	WHAT DEI ISSUES EXIST IN THE CONTEXT?	IDENTITY EXPERTISE RELEVANT	HOW MIGHT YOU LEVERAGE IDENTITY EXPERTISE TO CONTRIBUTE?
Team meetings	Minority; Latina	Race and gender disparity in how "office housework" like note-taking is assigned	Yes	Raise awareness of unequal assignments and suggest a rotating schedule
Web design team	Minority; bisexual	Website has several accessibility issues but no disabled developers	No	N/A
Client project	Majority; man	Men from client side are talking over women from our organization	Yes	Show respect for and call attention to the expertise of women colleagues
	Majority; _____			
	Majority; _____			
	Minority; _____			
	Minority; _____			

UNDERSTAND YOURSELF

EXPAND YOUR CAPACITY

RELY ON OTHERS

FIND YOUR PLACE

DIAGNOSE INEQUITY

CHAMPION INCLUSION

ADDRESS CONFLICT AND HARM

ORGANIZE A MOVEMENT

REIMAGINE SYSTEMS

ACHIEVE DEI

2. It can be tough to identify DEI issues in every context. If you had trouble identifying issues, or conversely if identifying issues was easy, why?

_____

_____

_____

_____

3. Reflect on the four opportunities you named. Out of these four, which opportunity feels the most approachable for you to actually take action on in the way you described?

_____

_____

_____

_____

4. What are the risks of taking action on this opportunity?

_____

_____

_____

_____

5. What are the benefits of taking action on this opportunity?

_____

_____

_____

_____

6. What steps would you follow in order to leverage your identity expertise in the opportunity you named? Describe a rough plan for how you might do so, thinking about who you'd talk with, what you'd say or do, where and when you'd engage, and how you'd reach out effectively.

_____

_____

_____

_____

_____

_____

7. This exercise focuses on the opportunities available to you, but your personal capacity is a larger predictor of whether you choose to act or not. Thinking only about yourself and your capacity, how will you choose when to act or not on an opportunity?

_____

_____

_____

_____

UNDERSTAND YOURSELF

EXPAND YOUR CAPACITY

RELY ON OTHERS

FIND YOUR PLACE

DIAGNOSE INEQUITY

CHAMPION INCLUSION

ADDRESS CONFLICT AND HARM

ORGANIZE A MOVEMENT

REIMAGINE SYSTEMS

ACHIEVE DEI

16

Explore Change-Making

Using power effectively in the context of DEI work means working alongside others, but this doesn't mean that everyone in a DEI movement does the exact same thing. Effective DEI movements are able to leverage their members to fill seven different roles, with each one substantially different from the others. The more we understand these roles, the more effectively we'll be able to fill them ourselves and strategize more broadly with other people in the DEI movements we build.

As collectives, we should strive to fill every one of these roles. But as individuals, putting our time and energy into playing a few roles well, rather than trying to play every role poorly, both helps us optimize our movement participation and also ensures that we as individuals don't burn out from overcommitment.

PRACTITIONER'S TIP

A group of specialists working well together has a higher potential for impact than one or two generalists wearing too many hats. This is true of many things, but it especially applies to DEI work. For passionate individuals, however, recognizing the value of specialists also means recognizing the inherent incompleteness of any one person—including yourself—attempting to take on all of this work at once. This is where humility is most valuable, and where the willingness to collaborate with other experts has enormous potential. Use this exercise to identify what niches you want to specialize in and identify the experts around you who you might tap for your DEI effort or movement.

LEARNING GOALS

- Learn about the seven types of change-making roles.
- Strategize on how your positionality, responsibilities, identities, and power impact the roles you might be most successful in.

UNDERSTAND YOURSELF

EXPAND YOUR CAPACITY

RELY ON OTHERS

FIND YOUR PLACE

DIAGNOSE INEQUITY

CHAMPION INCLUSION

ADDRESS CONFLICT AND HARM

ORGANIZE A MOVEMENT

REIMAGINE SYSTEMS

ACHIEVE DEI

INSTRUCTIONS

Learn about the seven types of change-making roles, key traits/skills of people who are often successful in those roles, and examples of each in action. Then, answer the exercise questions to identify the roles that are the best fit for you.

TYPE	ROLE	KEY TRAITS/SKILLS	EXAMPLE
Advocate	Increase movement momentum by raising awareness of an issue and firmly challenging the status quo	▪ Focus ▪ Honesty ▪ Empathy ▪ Bravery ▪ Communication	A junior employee raising awareness of ongoing worker mistreatment to force engagement on the issue
Educator	Inform and upskill current and potential members of movements with relevant information and expertise	▪ Patience ▪ Creativity ▪ Communication ▪ Listening ▪ Adaptability	An LGBTQ+ woman with experience starting several employee resource groups teaching colleagues how to do so
Organizer	Bring together a critical mass of people around a clearly articulated issue and clearly articulated requests/solutions	▪ Discipline ▪ Communication ▪ Collaboration ▪ Coordination ▪ Negotiation	A disabled manager bringing together a large coalition to create a set of internal closed-captioning standards
Strategist	Coordinate and inform movement direction, tactics, and solutions given a movement's power and resources	▪ Analysis ▪ Communication ▪ Adaptability ▪ Synthesis ▪ Curiosity	A VP drawing on 10+ years of experience with movements in the organization to suggest leaders to contact first
Backer	Formally and informally resource, support, and legitimize movements as part of a new and pending status quo	▪ Process orientation ▪ Translation ▪ Initiative ▪ Communication ▪ Perspective	A department head seen as part of the "old guard" of the organization reworking his yearly budget to include DEI
Builder	Create new policies, processes, practices, and products to execute on movement goals and embody new ideas	▪ Empathy ▪ Accountability ▪ Rigor ▪ Interdependence ▪ Creativity	A people operations professional who creates a new onboarding program to better support new hires
Reformer	Work within existing systems to make steady, incremental improvement to the status quo using feedback	▪ Listening ▪ Process orientation ▪ Patience ▪ Discipline ▪ Pragmatism	An executive setting increasingly ambitious DEI goals over time as previous goals are achieved

1. After reviewing the seven change-making roles and examples, brainstorm one DEI-related issue or movement (for example, addressing racist acts of exclusion or microaggressions; closing the gender pay gap; creating a safer environment for LGBTQ+ employees) and write it below.

_____

_____

_____

_____

The next several questions will ask you to imagine the roles you might play if you were involved in a movement or effort to address the issue you named.

2. What role(s) *most excite you* at this moment? Name no more than three. Why?

_____

_____

_____

_____

3. What role(s) could you *most realistically* see yourself filling with the skills and resources you have at this moment? Name no more than three. Why did you choose these role(s)?

_____

_____

_____

_____

4. What role(s) do you think you would be *hypothetically most effective in,* given your responsibility, identities, and opportunities, even if you're not able to realistically fill them in the moment? Name no more than three. Why did you choose these role(s)?

_____

_____

_____

_____

UNDERSTAND YOURSELF

EXPAND YOUR CAPACITY

RELY ON OTHERS

FIND YOUR PLACE

DIAGNOSE INEQUITY

CHAMPION INCLUSION

ADDRESS CONFLICT AND HARM

ORGANIZE A MOVEMENT

REIMAGINE SYSTEMS

ACHIEVE DEI

5. If there's a difference between your answers to questions 2, 3, and 4, what actions could you take to realize your answer to question 4 in practice?

_____

_____

_____

_____

6. Imagine that you were actually participating in the most effective role(s) you named. What actions would you engage in as part of those roles within a movement or DEI effort?

_____

_____

_____

_____

7. What role(s) would you be _least effective_ in, given your current responsibility, identities, and opportunities? Name no more than three. Why did you choose these role(s)?

_____

_____

_____

_____

8. What role(s) would be _most challenging_ for you, whether or not you would be effective in them? Name no more than three. Why did you choose these role(s)?

_____

_____

_____

_____

" PUTTING OUR TIME AND ENERGY INTO PLAYING A FEW ROLES WELL, RATHER THAN PLAYING EVERY ROLE POORLY, HELPS US OPTIMIZE OUR MOVEMENT PARTICIPATION AND ALSO ENSURES THAT WE DON'T BURN OUT FROM OVERCOMMITMENT.

DIAGNOSE INEQUITY

Identifying that inequity exists isn't difficult. Many of us, if we're existing in an environment that is disrespectful, toxic, discriminatory, or exclusionary, have a well-trained gut instinct that tells us that something just isn't right. This gut instinct is important—however, if we aim to be inclusive leaders and DEI practitioners, then we need to be able to do far more than "feel" the presence of inequity; we need to be able to prove it, not only to ourselves but to our peers and the leaders we work with.[22]

> " WE NEED TO DO OUR RESEARCH AND DIAGNOSE OUR OWN ENVIRONMENTS WITH A CRITICAL EYE AND GENUINE CURIOSITY ABOUT WHAT WE'LL FIND.

It starts with centering everything we do on outcomes. It's hard to move effectively from where we start unless we know where we're trying to end up. From there, we need to be able to see the big picture and think of our organizations from a systems lens—not just a collection of people, nor just a static set of policies, but as a dynamic, holistic, and complex system formed from people, practice, process, policy, culture, structure, and strategy. With this framework, we need to do our research and diagnose our own environments with a critical eye and genuine curiosity about what we'll find. These skills all feed into the same thing: the ability to confidently and compre-hensively answer the question, What is happening, why is it happening, and how do we make progress toward a more diverse, equitable, and inclusive status quo?

To some, this might feel like a need-lessly tedious effort, especially if the inequity we're aware of feels so glaringly obvious that "proving it" feels almost offensive. But skipping these steps is risky and can undermine even the most well-intentioned DEI effort. Rushing into action without setting a direction wastes precious trust, goodwill, and resources on "bridges to nowhere" that do much but achieve little. Eschewing a systemic approach for simplistic diagnoses can result in crude or "silver bullet" interven-tions that don't address the root causes behind inequities. Using our gut to diag-nose inequity, instead of more rigorous and accountable methods, risks both false positives (identifying inequities where none exist) and false negatives (failing to identify inequities that do exist). And failing to provide specifics around DEI work means that our odds of moving past a moral imperative into a truly operational one are low—making our odds of achieving success even lower.

These are the basic tools of what is typically now called a "data-driven approach," which in my opinion is the *only* approach that can create long-term, measurable, and accountable change.

22. Ma-Kellams, Christine, and Jennifer Lerner. "Trust your gut or think carefully? Examining whether an intuitive, versus a systematic, mode of thought produces greater empathic accuracy." *Journal of Personality and Social Psychology* 111, no. 5 (2016): 674. https://doi.org/10.1037/pspi0000063.

17

Operationalize Outcomes

"Greater diversity, equity, and inclusion" sounds good, but the truth is that by itself, it's not a particularly well-defined set of outcomes. It's an umbrella term: useful when discussing this work from a bird's-eye view, but not when getting into the operational weeds. There are striking similarities between how we might think about DEI outcomes and how we might think about *values*: they're all important, but the specifics of *which* we find most important tend to differ. If drilling down on our exact values helps us better understand ourselves, so too does drilling down on the exact DEI outcomes we want to achieve help us better engage in the work.[23]

PRACTITIONER'S TIP

There are as many different kinds of DEI outcomes as we can come up with, because ultimately the goal is for practitioners to be able to arrive at and articulate the customized, tailored outcomes unique to their organizations. To that end, treat this exercise as inspiration, but push yourself to go even further to define the outcomes your organization needs in no uncertain terms. The sample outcomes in this exercise were chosen from my own experiences, and I'm confident that they capture a large swath of DEI work succinctly enough to get people started. The challenge behind this exercise isn't finding outcomes that speak to you, but rather choosing the set that feels most reflective of your organization's priorities and challenges. Use this exercise to hone your focus and distill the abstract passion to do DEI into an operationalized set of outcomes tailored for your organization to strive for and achieve.

LEARNING GOALS

- Build awareness of what key DEI outcomes exist.
- Identify which key outcomes are most necessary to achieve in your organization.
- Reflect on what it means to center outcomes in your DEI efforts.

INSTRUCTIONS

Read the following list of 33 common DEI outcomes. Circle or mark the eight key outcomes that you think *best encapsulate the most urgent DEI needs for your community or organization.* Then list them in any order, and for each, share some thoughts on how this value shows up in your life in your thoughts and behaviors. Afterwards, answer the reflection questions.

Representational Parity A demographic composition at every level of seniority, within every department, and for every role that mirrors constituent demographics	**Representational Support** The collective sense that all are represented and supported by leaders, regardless of leaders' overall demographic composition	**Multicultural Environment** An environment with a high level of variety in people's identities, cultures, and backgrounds
Kindred Environment An environment with a high level of similarity in people's identities, cultures, and backgrounds	**Mixed Environment** An environment with pockets of high variety or similarity in people's identities, cultures, and backgrounds	**Accessible Environment** The collective sense of being able to participate fully in the workplace and in workplace processes as a result of having access needs met
Accountable Resolution Conflict resolution processes that are resolved fairly and satisfactorily, ensure accountability, and protect dignity for all parties	**Agency** The collective comfort and confidence to show up however authentically or not in an environment	**Authenticity** The collective expression of people's "authentic self" in an environment
Belonging The collective sense of feeling part of a greater whole and "part of the group" within an environment	**Community** The collective sense of having access to groups of people willing to provide mutual support and companionship	**Decision-Making** The collective sense of inclusion within decision-making processes and that shared feedback is valued and utilized
Enablement The collective sense of being equipped and resourced to successfully and sustainably fulfill responsibilities	**Engagement** High participation and buy-in for workplace processes and initiatives, and a sense of fulfillment from work	**Equitable Evaluation** An evaluation process that does not intentionally or unintentionally benefit some types of workers over others
Equitable Hiring A hiring process that does not intentionally or unintentionally benefit some types of candidates over others	**Equitable Promoting** A promotion process that does not intentionally or unintentionally benefit some types of candidates over others	**Ethical Behavior** Practices and relationships with institutions and workers that avoid nepotism, corruption, theft, and abuse
Fair Labor The collective sense of being rewarded fairly for the effort and quality of work being delivered, and treated without abuse or exploitation	**Inclusion** The collective sense of feeling respected and valued within an environment	**Non-exceptionalism** The ability for all workers to fulfill their responsibilities and be "average" without fear of repercussions

Privacy and Security The ability to control how information is collected and used, and the protections safeguarding this information	**Professional Growth** Tailored learning and development, challenging opportunities, and fair career progression for everyone	**Psychological Safety** An environment where people feel free to take risks, share critical feedback, and fail without fear of retaliation
Purpose The collective sense of contributing to an important purpose and mission through work	**Social Justice** Organizations leveraging their brand, platform, and resources to participate in social movements and achieve social justice	**Sustainability** The ability to operate without depleting natural resources needed to ensure a stable future
Transparency The collective understanding of an organization's operations, successes, and failures as a result of information sharing	**Trust** The collective sense of trusting the organization's leadership and processes to achieve what they purport to	**Universal Design** The collective sense of feeling included and able to utilize a product or service as intended
Well-Being An environment that sustains and supports the physical needs and mental health of everyone in it	**Work Flexibility** The collective sense of being able to work however, whenever, and wherever people want so long as work outcomes are achieved	**Work–Life Balance** The collective sense of feeling able to set boundaries between work and nonwork, and have those boundaries respected

EIGHT KEY OUTCOMES

1.

2.

3.

4.

5.

6.

7.

8.

UNDERSTAND YOURSELF

EXPAND YOUR CAPACITY

RELY ON OTHERS

FIND YOUR PLACE

DIAGNOSE INEQUITY

CHAMPION INCLUSION

ADDRESS CONFLICT AND HARM

ORGANIZE A MOVEMENT

REIMAGINE SYSTEMS

ACHIEVE DEI

REFLECTION QUESTIONS

1. How did you arrive at the eight outcomes you chose? How do you feel about this final list?

_____

_____

_____

_____

2. Of these eight, are there any that stand out as most urgent or highest priority for your organization or community? If so, which, and why?

_____

_____

_____

_____

3. Name an action your organization has taken in the last year that you think makes progress toward any of your key outcomes. Why do you think so?

_____

_____

_____

_____

4. Name an action your organization has taken in the last year that you think reverses, moves away from, or stalls progress on any of your key outcomes. Why do you think so?

_____

_____

_____

_____

5. Imagine that your organization's most senior leaders were to go through the same exercise. How might their eight key outcomes differ from yours, and why?

_____

_____

_____

_____

6. How might you build greater alignment and agreement on the key outcomes your organization should prioritize among all the people within it? Brainstorm some ideas.

_____

_____

_____

_____

NOTE

23. Zheng, Lily. "To Make Lasting Progress on DEI, Measure Outcomes." Harvard Business Review, January 27, 2023. https://hbr.org/2023/01/to-make-lasting-progress-on-dei-measure-outcomes.

UNDERSTAND YOURSELF

EXPAND YOUR CAPACITY

RELY ON OTHERS

FIND YOUR PLACE

DIAGNOSE INEQUITY

CHAMPION INCLUSION

ADDRESS CONFLICT AND HARM

ORGANIZE A MOVEMENT

REIMAGINE SYSTEMS

ACHIEVE DEI

18

Analyze Your Organization

A common sentiment in the DEI profession is "one-size-fits-all doesn't work." And while this statement is correct—interventions have to be tailored to the organization to be most effective—it's difficult to know exactly how to do the tailoring. That's because the prerequisite is understanding clearly how organizations differ from one another, not just in obvious ways like in size and industry, but also in their structure, culture, and strategy.

For inquiry and analysis, we can use structure, culture, and strategy as tools to help us "reverse engineer" why events happen the way they do. Outcomes emerge due to people's strategies—their choices. And those choices are heavily influenced by the systems of norms, incentives, rules, and expectations that collectively constitute structure and culture. If we can understand this black box of how outcomes emerge within environments, we can level up the DEI work we do with a far greater degree of intentionality and tactics.

PRACTITIONER'S TIP

While there will always be organizations in which DEI might feel easier vs. harder, there are no such things as "good" or "bad" structure, culture, or strategy. Analysis is *not* the same as judgment, and it is absolutely possible—if not preferable—to imagine DEI work as something that we can tailor to succeed within our organizations and environments, rather than thinking of it as a rigid agenda that we must tailor our environments to. Use this exercise as a framework for that analysis in any environment, from a three-person meeting to a global organization, whenever you're looking to strategize intentionally about DEI work.

LEARNING GOALS

- Understand what structure, culture, and strategy are and how they relate to outcomes.
- Use this framework to analyze an environment that you are personally familiar with.
- Gain experience modifying DEI work to succeed within an environment you understand the structure, culture, and strategy of.

UNDERSTAND YOURSELF

EXPAND YOUR CAPACITY

RELY ON OTHERS

FIND YOUR PLACE

DIAGNOSE INEQUITY

CHAMPION INCLUSION

ADDRESS CONFLICT AND HARM

ORGANIZE A MOVEMENT

REIMAGINE SYSTEMS

ACHIEVE DEI

INSTRUCTIONS

Learn about structure and culture from the charts on the opposite page, then use the checklist to informally analyze your own organization through these frameworks.

Structure and Culture

1. Name one environment whose structure and culture you'll reflect on for this exercise.

2. Check off the boxes in the following chart that correspond to the aspects of structure and culture in the environment you named.

ORGANIZATIONAL STRUCTURE AND CULTURE				
ASPECT	DESCRIPTION	LOW	MEDIUM	HIGH
STRUCTURE	**The rules, roles, and responsibilities that coordinate people.**			
Centralization	The degree to which decisions are made from the top down.			
Formalization	The degree to which organizational function is documented and follows strict rules			
Complexity	The degree to which organizations divide work across jobs, divisions, and locations			
CULTURE	**Shared assumptions and expectations for behavior in an environment**			
Power distance	The degree to which power differences are normalized and accepted			
Interdependence	The degree to which people see themselves as connected to a broader group			
Uncertainty avoidance	The degree to which uncertainty or ambiguity is avoided or devalued			
Failure avoidance	The degree to which failure or imperfection is avoided or devalued			

STRUCTURE
The set of rules, roles, and responsibilities that coordinate behavior and facilitate achieving the organization's goals

ASPECT	DEFINITION	EXAMPLES
Centralization[24]	The degree to which outcomes depend on controlled, powerful, top-down decisions	**High Centralization:** Command-and-control model with one executive making all important decisions **Low Centralization:** Higher education setting where every department or school is run differently
Formalization[25]	The degree to which formal rules, processes, and documentation govern behavior	**High Formalization:** Government bureaucracy, with most decisions requiring several formal steps **Low Formalization:** A group of friends that acts freely and without any concrete "rules"
Complexity[26]	The degree to which activities are split between people, jobs, roles, and locations	**High Complexity:** A global corporation with many layers of management and thousands of job titles **Low Complexity:** A small start-up with a few people, each covering for many different responsibilities

CULTURE
The shared but unspoken values, assumptions, and expectations for behavior, embodied by rituals, stories, and beliefs

ASPECT	DEFINITION	EXAMPLES
Power distance[27]	The degree to which a large disparity between the most and least powerful is acceptable	**High Power Distance:** A culture where hierarchies are expected, widespread, and valued **Low Power Distance:** A culture where leaders and employees are considered almost equals
Inter-dependence[28]	The degree to which people perceive their outcomes as interlinked vs. separate	**High Interdependence:** A culture exemplified by the saying "the loudest duck gets shot" **Low Interdependence:** A culture exemplified by the saying "the squeaky wheel gets the grease"
Uncertainty avoidance[29]	The degree to which people avoid vs. embrace uncertainty and ambiguity	**High Uncertainty Avoidance:** A culture that highly values predictability and fears change **Low Uncertainty Avoidance:** A culture that highly values innovation and adaptability
Failure avoidance[30]	The degree to which people avoid vs. embrace failure and imperfection	**High Failure Avoidance:** A culture where members suppress mistakes and value perfectionism **Low Failure Avoidance:** A culture where members value risk-taking and learning from mistakes

Strategy

While structure and culture play large parts in understanding outcomes, they aren't deterministic. Otherwise, we could easily predict any outcome using only the context of the structure and culture behind it. The wild card here is strategy.

While strategy is typically defined as the intentions of those with power, we can think of it more broadly and observably as "the choices that people with power make." And because everyone has some access to power, that means everybody has their own strategy. On the organizational level, we can think of strategy as the cumulative choices that people make. The choices of the most powerful people have a large bearing on organizational strategy, but everyone else's choices matter too—and if they clash, especially in ways that are surprising given the organization's structure and culture, that dynamic is important to note.

3. For your organization or environment, when and why would you say people make choices that conflict or go against the structure or culture? For example, in a high-failure-avoidance culture, when might people choose to admit failure, and why might they choose to do so?

---

4. People's choices can complement or conflict with each other. For example, if someone chooses to enforce a bureaucratic rule when they see it violated, another person can similarly enforce the rule—complementing the first person's choice—or choose to ignore that rule when they themselves see it violated—conflicting with the first person. Where in your experience do you see the most conflicting choices happening in your organization, and why do they occur?

UNDERSTAND YOURSELF

EXPAND YOUR CAPACITY

RELY ON OTHERS

FIND YOUR PLACE

DIAGNOSE INEQUITY

CHAMPION INCLUSION

ADDRESS CONFLICT AND HARM

ORGANIZE A MOVEMENT

REIMAGINE SYSTEMS

ACHIEVE DEI

5. Overall, if strategy is the net impact of the choices that people make—including clashing or contradicting choices—what would you say your organization's de facto DEI strategy is?

6. The more DEI work is tuned to complement an environment's structure, culture, and strategy, the more likely it is to succeed. How would you tune a complementary DEI initiative in your environment?

NOTES

24. Indeed Editorial Team. "Centralized vs. Decentralized Structures: 7 Key Differences." Indeed Career Guide, March 10, 2023. https://www.indeed.com/career-advice/career-development/centralized-vs -decentralized.

25. Assenova, Valentina A., and Olav Sorenson. "Legitimacy and the Benefits of Firm Formalization." Organization Science 28, no. 5 (2017): 804–818. https://doi.org/10.1287/orsc.2017.1146.

26. Tolbert, P. S., and R. H. Hall. Organizations: Structures, Processes and Outcomes. London: Routledge, 2015.

27. Hofstede, Geert. "Dimensionalizing cultures: The Hofstede model in context." Online Readings in Psychology and Culture 2, no. 1 (2011). https://doi.org/10.9707/2307-0919.1014.

28. Kafetsios, Konstantinos G., and Dritjon Gruda. "Interdependent followers prefer avoidant leaders: Followers' cultural orientation moderates leaders' avoidance relationships with followers' work outcomes." Frontiers in Communication 3 (2018). https://doi.org/10.3389/fcomm.2018.00009.

29. Snitker, Thomas Visby. "The Impact of Culture on User Research." In Handbook of Global User Research, 257–277. Elsevier, 2010.

30. Ocampo, Anna Carmella G., Lu Wang, Kohyar Kiazad, Simon Lloyd D. Restubog, and Neal M. Ashkanasy. "The relentless pursuit of perfectionism: A review of perfectionism in the workplace and an agenda for future research." Journal of Organizational Behavior 41, no. 2 (2020): 144–168. https://doi.org/10.1002/ job.2400.

19

Do Your Research

No matter how strong a feeling we have that inequities exist, those feelings are only as good as hunches unless we're able to clearly make our case with data: facts and information intentionally collected to gain knowledge and, in DEI, spanning everything from how many women occupy senior leadership positions to how confident LGBTQ+ employees feel in their managers. What turns any data into research is intentionally collecting, analyzing, and synthesizing that data into a clear set of findings that tell a story. Now, to set expectations—data science is clearly the realm of, well, data scientists. That said, anyone can learn the core mindset and principles needed to begin collecting and utilizing data effectively in their own environment. These foundational skills are useful for any data-driven effort,[31] whether undertaken by a formally trained data scientist utilizing machine learning, software modeling, and natural language processing or an enthusiast informally surveying their coworkers. With this framework as a foundation, you'll be able to get started using data effectively—and the sorts of advanced skills and knowledge bases you might gain from a formal class or degree program will only take you further.

PRACTITIONER'S TIP

"Research" takes many forms, and not just the ones that immediately come to mind. While big initiatives like a company-wide survey or network analyses of hundreds of thousands of emails are absolutely examples of using research for DEI work, any initiative can benefit from utilizing data effectively. It's the practice and discipline that comes with collecting and using data for research that's most valuable for practitioners to have. Use this exercise as structure and support whenever you want to take your intention to do DEI work to the next level with a more rigorous approach.

LEARNING GOALS

- Understand the five steps of effective data-driven efforts.
- Familiarize yourself with a framework for planning a research initiative.
- Strategize about how you might pursue a research initiative related to your DEI goals.

UNDERSTAND YOURSELF

EXPAND YOUR CAPACITY

RELY ON OTHERS

FIND YOUR PLACE

DIAGNOSE INEQUITY

CHAMPION INCLUSION

ADDRESS CONFLICT AND HARM

ORGANIZE A MOVEMENT

REIMAGINE SYSTEMS

ACHIEVE DEI

INSTRUCTIONS

Learn about the five steps of data-driven efforts from the following text, review the research framework and example, and follow the prompts to draft your own research initiative related to a DEI goal. Afterwards, answer the reflection questions.

The Five Steps of Data-Driven DEI Work

ARTICULATE YOUR GOALS

All data that's gathered should be gathered with a purpose, even if that purpose is an exploratory "let's see what's out there" before developing formal hypotheses. And if you're collecting data, it should be to answer a specific question that you couldn't easily answer without it. Articulating your goal in taking a data-driven approach isn't just responsible; it also holds those involved in the process accountable. Don't assume that people who support your data collection are all on the same page—specify and communicate the purpose of the research early on.

COLLECT DATA

Be creative about what you consider "data." Data can take a countless number of forms, from a collection of emails or chat messages, to employee survey data, to focus group or interview data, to aggregated turnover and retention data, and so on. It can be quantitative, qualitative, or a mix of the two. The type of data you collect and the way you collect it should be intentional, especially as data collection can often be a time- and resource-intensive undertaking. Let the goals of your data-driven project inform what kind of data you collect, from whom, in what ways, and for how long.

TEST YOUR HYPOTHESES

It can be easy—oftentimes, too easy—to cherry-pick our data and find exactly what we're looking for, which essentially reduces all of our effort to a glorified exercise in confirmation bias.[32] To avoid this, we need to carefully develop hypotheses or research questions and practice discipline in testing and challenging them, collecting additional data as needed. This makes it more likely that when we emerge with findings, these findings genuinely reflect insights from data rather than our personal biases or consequences of coincidence.

RECOGNIZE LIMITATIONS

It can be incredibly exciting to arrive at your first set of promising findings in any data-driven effort. Acting on this excitement, however, can easily result in overgeneralization, where a finding that may be true for a particular population in context is communicated as if it's true for many populations and across many contexts. These kinds of misleading distortions can be dangerous and result in solid research nevertheless doing harm due to overzealous follow-up. Slow down and recognize where your research hits its limit—if only to plan your future efforts.

TAKE ACTION

While being careful not to overstate findings, remember that the entire purpose of data collection is to take action. If you've carefully constructed your data-driven initiative, the last step is not communicating your findings, but using those findings to make progress toward your goals and taking action. That final task of follow-up requires leaders and powerful people who understood their role in the effort from the very beginning, and who are ready and willing to draw on the findings from research to solve problems and make the choices that matter.

Data-driven efforts start with knowing who we're focusing on, what aspect of their experience we're focusing on, and why. From there, we can create research questions: simple and specific questions that can be answered through research. These can be further refined into hypotheses: educated guesses that seek to answer research questions and that can be tested through a well-designed data collection strategy.

1. Review the following example of this framework in action, and answer the exercise questions.

WHAT What is the issue I want to look into through this effort?	WHO Which people or groups are affected by or involved in this issue?	WHY Why am I looking into this issue, what is the context, and what is my goal?
Workplace experiences with discrimination	LGBTQ+ staff in my organization; non-LGBTQ+ staff who may be engaging in discrimination	I've heard anecdotes of anti-LGBTQ+ discrimination and want to verify its existence, examine its prevalence, and possibly name its source.

RESEARCH QUESTIONS
How might I distill my objectives in this research into separate questions that I can answer?

1. Is anti-LGBTQ+ discrimination occurring?
2. How often does anti-LGBTQ+ discrimination occur?
3. Why does anti-LGBTQ+ discrimination occur?

HYPOTHESES
What are "educated guess" answers to my research questions that I can test?

1. Anti-LGBTQ+ discrimination is occurring, and it highly impacts LGBTQ+ employees.
2. Anti-LGBTQ+ discrimination occurs in both daily microaggressions and occasional, highly visible acts of blatant homophobia/transphobia from non-LGBTQ+ employees.
3. Anti-LGBTQ+ discrimination occurs because of an enabling organizational culture and the lack of clear consequences for misbehavior.

DATA COLLECTION STRATEGY
How might we collect data to test hypotheses and answer research questions?

1. Quantitative survey to all staff measuring key employee outcomes (engagement, belonging, access to opportunity, etc.), disaggregated by sexuality
2. Focus groups and interviews with LGBTQ+ employees or witnesses of discrimination
3. Exit interviews and discrimination complaints from LGBTQ+ employees

2. Name a DEI-related issue that you could use data to research and that you will focus on for this activity.

_____

_____

3. Answer the prompts to fill in the following empty chart for the issue you chose.

WHAT What is the issue I want to look into through this effort?	WHO Which people or groups are affected by or involved in this issue?	WHY Why am I looking into this issue, what is the context, and what is my goal?

RESEARCH QUESTIONS
How might I distill my objectives in this research into separate questions that I can answer?

HYPOTHESES
What are "educated guess" answers to my research questions that I can test?

DATA COLLECTION STRATEGY
How might we collect data to test hypotheses and answer research questions?

REFLECTION QUESTIONS

1. How does this process differ from what you might have done if told to "design a data-driven DEI initiative" yesterday?

_____

_____

_____

2. If you had the authority and resources to carry out the research project you described in your own organization, what would the process be like? What hiccups might occur?

_____

_____

_____

3. The framework outlined in this exercise ends with data collection. If you were to keep going with the effort you outlined, what would the next steps be? How would you carry this project to its conclusion?

_____

_____

_____

4. How likely is it that your organization would carry out the effort you outlined? What would need to change to make your organization more likely to undertake it, or do so more easily?

_____

_____

_____

NOTES

31. Authority Magazine Editorial Staff. "Author Lily Zheng on How to Use Data to Take Your Company to the Next Level." Medium, January 14, 2023. https://medium.com/authority-magazine/lily-zheng-on-how-to-use-data-to-take-your-company-to-the-next-level-64406e29326.

32. Schumm, Walter R. "Confirmation bias and methodology in social science: An editorial." _Marriage & Family Review_ 57, no. 4 (2021): 285–293. https://doi.org/10.1080/01494929.2021.1872859.

UNDERSTAND YOURSELF

EXPAND YOUR CAPACITY

RELY ON OTHERS

FIND YOUR PLACE

DIAGNOSE INEQUITY

CHAMPION INCLUSION

ADDRESS CONFLICT AND HARM

ORGANIZE A MOVEMENT

REIMAGINE SYSTEMS

ACHIEVE DEI

20

Tell the Story of "Why"

What many folks miss, especially those who consider themselves more adept at the data science side of this work, is that communicating and storytelling plays just as big a role as crunching the data itself.[33] Few people, whether senior leaders or junior employees, are motivated by a finding of "10% higher belonging scores for White men compared to Latina women" in isolation. The findings may be powerful, but building a sense of shared investment and responsibility requires going a step further and building a compelling narrative that will create change. Telling a compelling story that both draws people in and also stays true to your data and your research is a tough skill to master, but one way we can start is by grounding our story in "why": the step-by-step description of why the issue matters, why it arose, why we as practitioners are confident in our analysis, and why relevant parties need to take action.

PRACTITIONER'S TIP

Don't worry about writing the "perfect story"—there's no such thing. In fact, if which facts you highlight, your delivery, and other aspects of your story don't change across different audiences, you're missing out on the secret behind effective communication: it depends enormously on who you're communicating with and what your goals are. Note that this doesn't mean you should be making things up! When it comes to DEI work, the facts are the facts. But especially after a data-driven effort, there are *many, many, many* facts, and those you are trying to reach may not have an entire afternoon to hear you rattle off a list of findings. The art of storytelling is turning those facts into a compelling narrative, tailored to your audience, that gets them thinking and acting productively with the information. Use this exercise to hone facts into a tight narrative that helps you reach the people you need to.

LEARNING GOALS

- Practice communicating about DEI data and inequities in succinct, powerful ways.
- Integrate your intended outcomes, organizational analysis, and research.
- Reflect on how your communication and story might change across different audiences.

UNDERSTAND YOURSELF

EXPAND YOUR CAPACITY

RELY ON OTHERS

FIND YOUR PLACE

DIAGNOSE INEQUITY

CHAMPION INCLUSION

ADDRESS CONFLICT AND HARM

ORGANIZE A MOVEMENT

REIMAGINE SYSTEMS

ACHIEVE DEI

INSTRUCTIONS

All of the following questions will ask about one particular DEI-related issue or initiative that you choose to focus on. Follow the directions to develop your own complete DEI-related story. Afterwards, answer the reflection questions.

1. Choose one DEI-related issue or initiative to focus on throughout these exercises—it does not need to be one for which you've gathered data. Consider reusing an issue you used for the other exercises in this section.

_____

_____

_____

_____

_____

2. For this issue or initiative, what outcomes are you trying to achieve by telling a story?

_____

_____

_____

_____

_____

3. Pick one person or group that you might tell a story to about your issue or initiative in order to achieve the outcomes you listed for question 2. They might be a peer, a senior leader, an acquaintance, or a news publication, for example. Tailor your answers to the following questions to the audience you name here.

_____

_____

_____

_____

_____

4. The first "why" we need to answer is, Why does this issue matter? In your answer to this question, consider naming "who" the issue impacts, and "what" they experience. Consider drawing from your answers on Who and What in the research framework chart in Exercise 19.

_____

_____

_____

_____

5. The next "why" is, Why did this issue arise? In your answer to this question, provide an answer drawing either from real data analysis you conducted (optional) or a temporary answer using hypotheses, or educated guesses. Consider drawing from your analyses of organizational structure, culture, and strategy from Exercise 18.

_____

_____

_____

_____

6. Afterwards, we need to answer, Why are we confident in our analysis? In your answer to this question, provide an answer drawing either from your real research (optional) or a temporary answer using what you might hypothetically do. Consider drawing from The Five Steps of Data-Driven DEI Work in Exercise 19.

_____

_____

_____

7. The final "why" is, Why, and how, should you take action? This answer should connect in some way to your answers to the questions, Why does this issue matter? and Why did this issue arise? In your answer, consider also drawing on your knowledge of your organization and your audience, and recommending solutions that address specific factors you identified as contributing to the issue.

_____

_____

_____

_____

UNDERSTAND YOURSELF

EXPAND YOUR CAPACITY

RELY ON OTHERS

FIND YOUR PLACE

DIAGNOSE INEQUITY

CHAMPION INCLUSION

ADDRESS CONFLICT AND HARM

ORGANIZE A MOVEMENT

REIMAGINE SYSTEMS

ACHIEVE DEI

8. Finally, put it all together. Building on your responses to questions 4–7, tell a per-suasive story for your target audience with the goal of achieving the outcomes you named. There are many ways you might build on your previous answers: you might connect the issue to the audience's existing priorities, share an emotional story about who the issue affects, link the root cause of the issue to other issues the audience cares about, dive into the methodology used to arrive at your findings, or frame your audience's participation as mutually beneficial, for example.

_____

_____

_____

_____

_____

_____

_____

_____

_____

_____

_____

_____

_____

_____

_____

_____

_____

_____

REFLECTION QUESTIONS

1. What was challenging for you while putting together your story? What additional elements did you insert in your answer to exercise question 8, and why?

_____

_____

_____

_____

2. How do you think your audience would respond to this story? Are there ways you could have tailored it even more?

_____

_____

_____

3. Put yourselves in the mindset of an audience member who may not have fully bought in before hearing your story. What additional things might they be looking for before taking action other than this story? How might those things change your initiative or effort?

_____

_____

_____

4. Imagine that you did the same exercise for a very different audience, and name that audience. What aspects of your story would you emphasize, de-emphasize, introduce, or take away, and why?

_____

_____

_____

_____

NOTE

33. Rodriguez, Jimmy. "6 Steps to Persuasive Data Storytelling (+Examples)." WordStream, March 16, 2022. https://www.wordstream.com/blog/ws/2021/05/27/data-storytelling.

UNDERSTAND YOURSELF

EXPAND YOUR CAPACITY

RELY ON OTHERS

FIND YOUR PLACE

DIAGNOSE INEQUITY

CHAMPION INCLUSION

ADDRESS CONFLICT AND HARM

ORGANIZE A MOVEMENT

REIMAGINE SYSTEMS

ACHIEVE DEI

CHAMPION INCLUSION

Diagnosing inequity is powerful work, but it can also feel abstract, intellectual, and cerebral at times. It's not enough for practitioners and inclusive leaders to intellectualize about DEI work if they're not able to make the very real people in front of them feel safe, included, and valued in their own environments. This is easier said than done, especially if the people we're working with have as much variation in their identities and experiences as exist in the world.

> **IF WE FAIL TO UNDERSTAND THE SUBTLETIES OF HOW, WHEN, AND WHY TO USE OUR POWER AND INFLUENCE, WE'LL FIND OURSELVES PART OF THE PROBLEM RATHER THAN THE SOLUTION.**

Championing inclusion is the interpersonal, human side of this work, and it requires getting good at rapidly gaining and integrating new knowledge. It requires that we become adept at creating and maintaining an inclusive culture that energizes and protects those around us. We need to recognize too that championing inclusion is often less about making ourselves the "champion," but more about using our power to empower others' self-determination and community-building and, when needed, taking a stand on issues that matter—not for our own self-promotion, but to make real our commitment to the communities we're working with and on behalf of.

This is delicate work, and it's easy to misalign our well-intended efforts. If we lean too hard in the direction of cultural humility, "trying to accept that we'll never learn everything" can turn into "giving up on learning anything." If we lean too hard in the direction of cultural competence, we'll be too terrified to engage with anything new until we've learned literally everything to know. Both extremes harm those we're engaging with, who don't want to be used as "learning moments," "reminders of humility," or "challenges to overcome." If we're not able to create inclusive cultures around us, that's the fastest way to get accused of performative DEI: talking the talk, but when the rubber hits the road being unable to embody inclusion in practice. And finally, if we fail to understand the subtleties of how, when, and why to use our power and influence, we'll find ourselves part of the problem— making DEI about us when it needs to be about others, or failing to speak up exactly when our influence is most needed—rather than the solution.

Building our own abilities as leaders to navigate these complexities and succeed is truly an example of "lifelong learning." But don't mistake a skill that takes a lifetime to master for one that's hard to become proficient in. Remember the metaphor of learning a language: what feels slow and clunky at first quickly feels easier and more comfortable, especially with someone to practice with. Championing inclusion is no different.

21

Learn to Learn

I'm sure you've seen it or experienced it before: the almost painfully awkward attempts, typically from a person with more privileged social identities, to engage with someone with different life experiences. The "Google-able" questions, embarrassing assumptions, offensive jokes, and faux pas. More importantly, their impact on the person these uninformed comments are directed at: not just embarrassment, but exclusion, disrespect, and harm. Most people, even if they flub their initial attempts to engage, improve over time if they keep trying. But this "learning" almost always comes at the expense of their target's sense of inclusion, respect, and belonging, because they know no other way to learn about difference than to crash into it.

Mistakes are human. But *learning how to learn* about difference can ensure we minimize our mistakes and can rebound gracefully from those we make. The key is simple in concept but challenging in practice: when you encounter difference, do some basic research on your own before asking a person what questions remain. This simple idea will make it far easier to learn while maintaining respect and inclusion.

> **PRACTITIONER'S TIP**
>
> It may feel odd at first, when meeting a person from a culture we know little about, to disengage with them to "do our own homework." They're right in front of us, so why not ask to learn more, right? But doing so, especially if we swarm them with uninformed and basic questions about their identity or background, often causes them to feel like we're treating them like exotic curiosities. The more we put the onus on ourselves to learn about culture and identity *before questioning the individual in front of us*, the more space we make for them to engage with us on their own terms.[34] Use this exercise to gain greater perspective about unfamiliar identities and guide your personal learning about any dimension of difference.

LEARNING GOALS

- Learn principles of self-directed learning to do your research before directing so-called Google-able questions at someone different from you.
- Practice doing research on an identity or culture you're less familiar with.
- Use your understanding of your own culture to inform how you might learn about others'.

UNDERSTAND YOURSELF

EXPAND YOUR CAPACITY

RELY ON OTHERS

FIND YOUR PLACE

DIAGNOSE INEQUITY

CHAMPION INCLUSION

ADDRESS CONFLICT AND HARM

ORGANIZE A MOVEMENT

REIMAGINE SYSTEMS

ACHIEVE DEI

INSTRUCTIONS

Read Learning about Difference to grasp the principles, then answer the exercise questions to engage in self-directed research about familiar and unfamiliar cultures. Afterwards, answer the reflection questions.

Learning about Difference

When engaging with a person from a culture unfamiliar to you, you can use the following rough rules/principles to learn respectfully about their culture or identity.

1. Recognize the context and act accordingly. Some environments are more or less conducive to interpersonal learning. For example, if it's a Q and A session specifically intended to learn about identity, ask away. If it's a work meeting, a generic networking event, or otherwise unrelated to identity-related questioning, avoid this level of public questioning.

2. Within the context, pause and follow the lead of people from that community. If they are not proactively bringing up their culture, don't mention it. If they are proactively discussing the topic you want to learn about, you can politely ask questions at a similar level of intimacy.

3. Outside of the context, do your own research. Engage in a web search or otherwise draw from a range of sources to do personal learning. Keep in mind the following tips:

- Prioritize information created by the community. Start your learning by seeking out the perspectives of those inside the community themselves, rather than outsiders.
- There is no one single or perfect representative of a culture. Seek out a variety of perspectives from across the community to inform your learning, even if they may contradict each other—nuance lives in these contradictions.
- Don't reinvent the wheel. You are not the first person to try to learn about the culture or identity you're curious about. Take your time to find resources geared toward beginners.
- Embrace multimedia learning. Seek out content documentaries, internet articles, books, music and poetry, podcasts, short form videos, and many other formats.
- Listen and observe. Don't jump into action. If you skim a video and want to ask a question in the comments section, pause, and before you ask, rewatch the video. Skim the comments section for anyone else who may have asked the same question.

4. Figure out what, if anything, you still want to ask. Many times, self-directed research will answer your questions. If not, answer for yourself what you want to ask this person, and why.

5. Check their boundaries. In a neutral context (one in which there is no important activity going on) ask, "May I ask you a question about _____?" If they say no, thank them and respect their boundaries. If they say yes, thank them and then clearly communicate what kind of and how many questions you want to ask.

6. Ask respectfully. To introduce your question(s), briefly mention your own self-directed research and identify what you're looking for more information on. Then ask your question(s), thank them for their answer(s), and move on.

REFLECTION QUESTIONS

1. Which of these steps or principles might be most challenging for you? Why?

_____

_____

_____

_____

2. If anyone has ever engaged with you to learn about an identity or culture you have experience with, did they engage respectfully? Which of these principles did they use (or not)?

_____

_____

_____

_____

3. Choose *two* identity- or culture-related topics to focus on for the rest of the questions in this exercise. Purposefully pick one identity or culture that you are *not* a part of or familiar with—a beginner on—and one identity or culture that you *are* a part of and are familiar with—an expert on. Write the topics you chose in the following boxes.

Beginner	Expert

UNDERSTAND YOURSELF

EXPAND YOUR CAPACITY

RELY ON OTHERS

FIND YOUR PLACE

DIAGNOSE INEQUITY

CHAMPION INCLUSION

ADDRESS CONFLICT AND HARM

ORGANIZE A MOVEMENT

REIMAGINE SYSTEMS

ACHIEVE DEI

4. Find basic information about both topics you chose. Start off with a basic web search, if able, or find a book that might have relevant information. Some questions you might want to ask include, What does it mean to be _____? What makes some-one _____? and What are some basic statistics about _____? where the blank space refers to the topics you chose. For now, only note down information you find in this first search, without relying on prior knowledge.

Beginner	Expert

5. Then, look for more in-depth information. Some questions you might want to ask include, What are some common misconceptions about _____? What are some debates about _____ issues? How do you engage respectfully with _____ people? and What is the history of _____ culture? where the blank space refers to the topics you chose.

Beginner	Expert

6. Thinking about the topic you chose that you *already* knew about or were an expert in, how accurate would you say the content you saw was?

_____

_____

_____

_____

7. If you were to teach somebody the basics about that topic, what other instructions might you have given to help them learn what was missing?

_____

_____

_____

_____

8. Based on your answer to question 7, what self-directed learning sources would you seek out on the *beginner* topic before reaching out to a person you know from that community?

_____

_____

_____

_____

NOTE

34. Zheng, Lily. "It's Not Your Coworkers' Job to Teach You about Social Issues." Harvard Business Review, August 27, 2021. https://hbr.org/2019/07/its-not-your-coworkers-job-to-teach-you-about-social-issues.

UNDERSTAND YOURSELF

EXPAND YOUR CAPACITY

RELY ON OTHERS

FIND YOUR PLACE

DIAGNOSE INEQUITY

CHAMPION INCLUSION

ADDRESS CONFLICT AND HARM

ORGANIZE A MOVEMENT

REIMAGINE SYSTEMS

ACHIEVE DEI

22

Change Culture

In the Diagnose Inequity section, you learned that culture is "the shared but unspoken values, assumptions, and expectations for behavior, embodied by rituals, stories, and beliefs" and how to analyze the culture of an environment. But culture isn't just something we can feel—it's something we can shape and mold through our own actions. Not convinced? On the level of our organizations, culture can be hard to shift, that's true. But every department or unit in an organization has its own culture, and influencing that is a little easier. Every group of employees has its own culture, and influencing that is even easier. Every team, and even every pair of people, has its own culture, and influencing that is as easy as it gets.

Thinking of culture as something that we don't just passively exist within but instead can actively shape, even if we're working within larger contexts that are hard to change on our own, gives us a new avenue to use our power and influence to create inclusion. Doing this on the smallest level possible—with *microcultures*—is the starting point to level up our impact.[35]

> **PRACTITIONER'S TIP**
>
> The aspects of culture that make it hardest to understand—namely, that it's often unspoken and rarely ever defined—also give us as practitioners some of the most useful tools to influence it ourselves. The right leader, taking the right action in the right moment, can create an enduringly inclusive culture with very little effort. The requirements to achieve this kind of impact are the knowledge of how to establish culture, the foresight to know when moments of opportunity arise, and the confidence to decisively take action at the right moment. Use this exercise to fill the first requirement, and continue using it to gain the experience needed to fill the other two. The more time you spend creating and shifting microculture through your own actions, the more consistently you'll be able to create the change you seek.

LEARNING GOALS

- Acquire new strategies for shaping microcultures.
- Analyze the gap between existing microcultures around you and a more equitable or inclusive ideal.
- Apply your knowledge to brainstorm strategies to shape the microcultures around you.

UNDERSTAND YOURSELF

EXPAND YOUR CAPACITY

RELY ON OTHERS

FIND YOUR PLACE

DIAGNOSE INEQUITY

CHAMPION INCLUSION

ADDRESS CONFLICT AND HARM

ORGANIZE A MOVEMENT

REIMAGINE SYSTEMS

ACHIEVE DEI

INSTRUCTIONS

Learn what strategies are effective for shaping microcultures, and answer the exercise questions. Then, follow the prompts to fill out the chart on microcultures in your own environment.

Strategies for Shifting Microcultures

A microculture is culture—defined by a shared set of expectations, assumptions, rules, and beliefs—on a small scale. It can be the shared expectations between two or three friends in a friend group. It can be the unspoken rules on a sports field or court. It can be the shared beliefs about what constitutes a "successful" meeting among a small team. Just as culture drives what behaviors are seen as normal or not, microculture does the same. But unlike broader culture, which is often created over a long period of time and requires the rough agreement of many people, microcultures can be created or changed quickly, and only require the rough agreement of the handful of people within them. How? Through several different strategies.

GET THERE FIRST

When a relationship of any kind begins, there's enormous potential for the first few expectations, informal rules, and beliefs to anchor the culture. By being there from the beginning, you can influence how a microculture begins.

CHANGE THE ROUTINE

A little-known way to change people's behavior is to change the routines they go through. Simply including a five-minute "gratitude" agenda item during a weekly meeting, for example, may normalize the behavior of gratitude and shift the culture accordingly.

SHAPE THE CHOICES

One way to reduce unwanted behaviors is to intentionally shape the options offered to people. Telling a team to share feedback during *either* a Monday *or* a Friday meeting, for example, may lower the chance that they don't share feedback at all.

USE SOCIAL INCENTIVES

People are highly attuned to incentives, especially social rewards. Explicitly recognizing, celebrating, and giving positive attention to a teammate who makes a mistake and learns from it, for example, may lower a team's fear of failure.

CREATE SHARED COMMITMENT

When people make a shared public commitment to replace an existing behavior, start a new behavior, or both—and importantly, expect mutual accountability from each other to maintain the changed behaviors—that can result in culture change.

1. Name *one* context, group, or relationship to focus on for this exercise. It can be a team, group of colleagues, or even your relationship with one other person.

_____

_____

2. Which of the strategies just described feels the *easiest* for you to use in your own context?

_____

_____

_____

_____

3. Which of those strategies feels the *hardest* for you to use in your own context?

_____

_____

_____

_____

4. Remember that culture is "the shared but unspoken values, assumptions, and expectations for behavior, embodied by rituals, stories, and beliefs." List some of the current cultural ideas present in the context you named. For example, they may include the value of hard work and productivity, the assumption that health always comes before work, or the expectation that all decisions go through a supervisor before getting made.

_____

_____

_____

_____

UNDERSTAND YOURSELF

EXPAND YOUR CAPACITY

RELY ON OTHERS

FIND YOUR PLACE

DIAGNOSE INEQUITY

CHAMPION INCLUSION

ADDRESS CONFLICT AND HARM

ORGANIZE A MOVEMENT

REIMAGINE SYSTEMS

ACHIEVE DEI

5. Now, thinking more broadly, brainstorm some values, assumptions, and expectations for behavior that you might find in a *diverse, equitable, and inclusive environment*. For example, these might include the assumption that when interpersonal harm happens, people take responsibility for making it right.

_____

_____

_____

6. Putting your answers to question 4 in the leftmost column and question 5 in the middle column, follow the prompts to strategize about how you might influence *three aspects* of your context's current culture toward the values, assumptions, and expectations you brainstormed. An example is included.

CURRENT CULTURE What is the aspect of this culture that exists at present?	DEI-SUPPORTIVE CULTURE How might this aspect look if it were adapted to better support DEI?	STRATEGY How might I influence the current culture toward a more DEI-supportive culture through my own actions?
People don't want to make mistakes, and don't engage with DEI topics.	Greater willingness to make mistakes that result in learning, and greater engagement with DEI.	*Use social incentives* to celebrate mistakes that result in learning. *Use shared commitments* to take greater risks *and* own the impacts of mistakes.

NOTE

35. Gallo, Amy, Amit Maimon, and Ron Ashkenas. "Keep Your Company's Toxic Culture from Infecting Your Team." Harvard Business Review, June 13, 2019. https://hbr.org/2019/04/keep-your-companys-toxic -culture-from-infecting-your-team.

" THE RIGHT LEADER,
TAKING THE RIGHT ACTION IN
THE RIGHT MOMENT,
CAN CREATE AN ENDURINGLY
INCLUSIVE CULTURE
WITH VERY LITTLE EFFORT.

23

Empower Others

The most effective and inclusive leaders aren't "inclusion champions" because they're magnanimous dictators. If they have reputations as inclusive leaders, it's because they use their access to power to remove barriers, interrupt inequitable systems, and actively empower others. Learning to lead in this way means getting rid of the notion of the traditional command-and-control style of leadership, in which leaders are owed the absolute obedience of those who report to them, and owe absolute obedience to those they report to. Inclusive leaders who lead by empowering others still use their power, but they use it instead to actively seek out and remove external and internal obstacles to their teams' success, secure the resources their teams need to thrive, protect their teams from distractions, and serve as "translators" to turn the demands of the organization into parsable information their teams can act on.[36] Even if you don't have formal authority as a manager, you can learn and practice the skill of using your own power to empower others.

> **PRACTITIONER'S TIP**
>
> Empowering others is both an art and a science. Even though it's contrasted with command-and-control styles of leadership, good empowerment is far more than simply being hands-off. The goal of an empowering style of leadership is ultimately the same as other styles: to ensure people accomplish what's expected of them. It's the "how" that varies: empowering styles focus on giving people the resources and support they need, the structure and guidance they need, and the power and autonomy they need. The common theme is working *together* with others to determine what *they* need, rather than assuming a one-size-fits-all approach or imposing our personal preferences. Use this exercise to plan out how you might use your own power to empower others by removing obstacles in any context

LEARNING GOALS

- Make connections between your power within a context, the obstacles in that context, and how you might utilize your power to empower others.
- Plan how you might center the needs of those you want to empower before taking action.
- Reflect on how you might mitigate some of the common failure modes of empowerment.

UNDERSTAND YOURSELF

EXPAND YOUR CAPACITY

RELY ON OTHERS

FIND YOUR PLACE

DIAGNOSE INEQUITY

CHAMPION INCLUSION

ADDRESS CONFLICT AND HARM

ORGANIZE A MOVEMENT

REIMAGINE SYSTEMS

ACHIEVE DEI

INSTRUCTIONS

Answer the exercise questions to reflect on an environment where you might empower others, and review the types of power and responsibility, as well as example answers. Then, answer the reflection questions.

1. Name an environment or context that you will use for this exercise, and people within the context you want to empower.

2. Empowering others first requires that we understand the needs of those we're working with. What are their common goals, and what do they care about achieving?

3. What issues are they facing within the context? How might addressing these issues increase their ability to achieve their own goals?

Power and responsibility make it possible to empower others, and the types of power and types of responsibility are listed here.

TYPES OF POWER	
Formal	The right or authority to request behavior from another
Reward	The ability to promise compensation to influence behavior
Coercive	The ability to threaten punishment to influence behavior
Expert	The ability to influence behavior by being seen as possessing greater expertise
Information	The ability to influence behavior by possessing greater information
Referent	The ability to build rapport and influence behavior through charisma

TYPES OF RESPONSIBILITY	
Task responsibility	The responsibility to execute a defined task
Outcome responsibility	The responsibility to ensure a specific end result or outcome
Stewardship responsibility	The responsibility to define, represent, or safeguard important systems, processes, or ideals, often from the top down
Shared responsibility	The collective responsibility to maintain important systems, processes, or ideals, often from the bottom up

4. List the type(s) of power and responsibility you have access to in the context you named, and describe how they manifest.

_____

_____

_____

_____

5. Now, put it all together to plan out how you might empower others. How might you use *your power* to meet people's needs in the context by removing or addressing *obstacles*? An example is provided.

CONTEXT What is the environment you will work within?	YOUR POWER What kinds of power do you have access to?	OBSTACLES IN CONTEXT What obstacles do people in the context experience?	EMPOWERING OTHERS How might you use your power to remove or address obstacles in the context?
Team meetings	*Referent* power (highly respected), *outcome responsibility* as timekeeper	Some team members consistently speak over others and monopolize speaking time.	Keep track of speaking time during meetings; halfway through, encourage thoughts from different people as part of the time check.

An empty version of this chart is included to better facilitate your thinking. After thinking, write out your plan.

CONTEXT What is the environment you will work within?	YOUR POWER What kinds of power do you have access to?	OBSTACLES IN CONTEXT What obstacles do people in the context experience?	EMPOWERING OTHERS How might you use your power to remove or address obstacles in the context?

REFLECTION QUESTIONS

1. Think about a time when someone tried to use their power or responsibilities to remove an obstacle you were facing and *did it well*. What happened, and what was the impact on you?

_____

_____

_____

_____

2. Think about a time when someone tried to use their power or responsibilities to remove an obstacle you were facing and *did it poorly*. What happened, and what was the impact on you?

_____

_____

_____

_____

3. What are some potential outcomes of intervening in the ways you outlined? List at least one positive and one negative outcome.

_____

_____

_____

4. How might you make it more likely that positive outcomes result from your actions?

_____

_____

_____

UNDERSTAND YOURSELF

EXPAND YOUR CAPACITY

RELY ON OTHERS

FIND YOUR PLACE

DIAGNOSE INEQUITY

CHAMPION INCLUSION

ADDRESS CONFLICT AND HARM

ORGANIZE A MOVEMENT

REIMAGINE SYSTEMS

ACHIEVE DEI

5. This exercise focused on one context and one obstacle, but it can be applied to many contexts and many different obstacles within a context. What are some other contexts or obstacles you could imagine using this approach to empower people in?

_____

_____

_____

_____

NOTE

36. Letizia, Angelo. *Using Servant Leadership: How to Reframe the Core Functions of Higher Education.* Rutgers University Press, 2018.

" EMPOWERING STYLES FOCUS ON WORKING *TOGETHER* WITH OTHERS TO DETERMINE WHAT *THEY* NEED, RATHER THAN ASSUMING A ONE-SIZE-FITS-ALL APPROACH OR IMPOSING OUR PERSONAL PREFERENCES.

24

Use Your Visibility

It would be easy to assume that a leader who focused on empowering others wouldn't spend much time in the spotlight as the center of attention. However, the most inclusive leaders are actually quite comfortable in the spotlight—but they choose these moments of visibility intentionally. When they do draw attention, it's not to promote themselves but to instead use their power and platform to take a stand on important issues. By putting their weight behind an issue that has less visibility, understanding, or support, but that significantly affects their teams' well-being, success, and inclusion, leaders put pressure on the status quo to create a new normal. To get there, of course, leaders have to have achieved the prerequisites: they have to know how to learn about their teams' issues, know how to create and sustain culture, and regularly empower others. The end goal is being a leader who is able to recognize when the time comes to take a stand, feels confident taking risks even if that might ruffle feathers, and takes decisive action to challenge norms and create a new, more equitable and inclusive status quo.

PRACTITIONER'S TIP

The power of using visibility to take a stand is shifting people's perception of what is "acceptable" or "normal." For example, a policy suggestion that might seem impossible or decades away might almost overnight become seen as possible or even reasonable, if a well-respected and powerful leader adopts it for their own and takes a stand on its usage. The secret behind using this skill effectively is framing: the more a leader is able to present their stance on an issue as "normal" or "commonplace"—and the more a leader is able to present the status quo as "unusual" or "unreasonable"—the more powerfully and widely it will resonate. Use this exercise when empowerment isn't enough and you need to use your power as a leader more directly to challenge an entrenched culture, policy, process, or practice.

LEARNING GOALS

- Understand the three stages of visibility leaders can utilize to challenge the status quo.
- Brainstorm what the three stages of visibility look like in practice for a specific context, and reflect on their combined impact.
- Plan out what it would take to prepare for and utilize the three stages of visibility.

INSTRUCTIONS

Learn about the three stages of visibility required to change a norm, and answer the exercise questions to brainstorm and plan how you might do so in your own context.

Changing Norms by Using Your Visibility

In environments where the status quo is deeply entrenched, working on the level of individual learning, microcultures, and empowerment may simply not be enough to make lasting change. In these situations, leaders and others with power must take stronger steps to change norms. By taking stands on important issues—and doing so in progressively stronger and bolder ways—leaders can use their power to create new ways of thinking, doing, and interpreting that constitute a new normal. Leaders can employ three stages of visibility to do so:

STAGE 1: CHALLENGE THE NORM

The first stage of visibility that leaders can achieve is simply putting forward the idea that the status quo isn't the only reasonable way to be and introducing an alternative. Often, this takes the form of a simple idea that nonetheless can feel shocking because it upends "conventional" wisdom. For example, in a traditional workplace, a leader can publicly assert that "we can and should work remotely" and refuse to back down even in the face of uproar.

STAGE 2: TAKE BOLD ACTION

The second stage of visibility that leaders can achieve is taking the first step to embody the new norm they aim to create with a behavior that would be "common-place" if the norm were different but nonetheless feels like a violation of the current order. For example, in the same workplace, all employees who report to that leader can be allowed to work remotely for a period of time with the leader's personal promise that they will take on any criticism or risk for doing so.

STAGE 3: DOUBLE DOWN

The final stage of visibility that leaders can achieve is doubling down on their action, often in the face of continued resistance, after demonstrating the value of the new norm. The goal is to celebrate the possibility of a new normal and signal strongly to others that this new norm is not only possible, but maybe even better than the old normal. For example, in the same workplace, productivity numbers and client satisfaction data can be released alongside a new policy for the team protecting remote working indefinitely.

1. Identify an entrenched aspect of your context's culture, strategy, policies, processes, or practices that may resist casual attempts to change. What makes it so entrenched?

_____

_____

_____

_____

2. Who is disproportionately and negatively affected by this aspect, and how? Focus on equity and inclusion-related disparities and negative outcomes.

_____

_____

_____

_____

3. What do these people and communities advocate as a replacement to improve their equity and inclusion-related outcomes? What makes it better?

_____

_____

_____

_____

Recall the types of power and responsibility.

TYPES OF POWER	
Formal	The right or authority to request behavior from another
Reward	The ability to promise compensation to influence behavior
Coercive	The ability to threaten punishment to influence behavior
Expert	The ability to influence behavior by being seen as possessing greater expertise
Information	The ability to influence behavior by possessing greater information
Referent	The ability to build rapport and influence behavior through charisma

UNDERSTAND YOURSELF

EXPAND YOUR CAPACITY

RELY ON OTHERS

FIND YOUR PLACE

DIAGNOSE INEQUITY

CHAMPION INCLUSION

ADDRESS CONFLICT AND HARM

ORGANIZE A MOVEMENT

REIMAGINE SYSTEMS

ACHIEVE DEI

TYPES OF RESPONSIBILITY	
Task responsibility	The responsibility to execute a defined task
Outcome responsibility	The responsibility to ensure a specific end result or outcome
Stewardship responsibility	The responsibility to define, represent, or safeguard important systems, processes, or ideals, often from the top down
Shared responsibility	The collective responsibility to maintain important systems, processes, or ideals, often from the bottom up

4. List the type(s) of power and responsibility you have access to, and describe how they manifest.

_____

_____

_____

_____

5. In what context(s) are you most able to leverage this power to use your visibility to take a stand?

_____

_____

_____

_____

6. In the context you named, how might you take a stand to achieve *stage 1: challenge the norm*, on the issue marginalized communities are advocating about? What would you say or do?

_____

_____

_____

_____

7. In the context you named, how might you take a stand to achieve *stage 2: take bold action*, on the issue marginalized communities are advocating about? What would you say or do?

---

8. In the context you named, how might you take a stand to achieve *stage 3: double down* on the issue marginalized communities are advocating about? What would you say or do?

---

9. When you take a stand, conflict, resistance, and criticism can be a common reaction. What are some of the reactions you imagine you might receive to any of the stands you take?

---

10. What responses or replies can you prepare in order to respond best to these reactions? In general, how will you ensure that you are able to continue through the three stages of taking a stand without getting shut down?

UNDERSTAND YOURSELF

EXPAND YOUR CAPACITY

RELY ON OTHERS

FIND YOUR PLACE

DIAGNOSE INEQUITY

CHAMPION INCLUSION

ADDRESS CONFLICT AND HARM

ORGANIZE A MOVEMENT

REIMAGINE SYSTEMS

ACHIEVE DEI

ADDRESS CONFLICT AND HARM

No matter how hard we try as practitioners, our actions will not result in the complete absence of harm. In the time it takes to change deep-rooted inequities in our organizations and environments, those inequities and the way they manifest in our interpersonal relationships, experiences with systems and structures, and shared expectations and values will likely continue causing harm. People will say the wrong thing, behave in ways that

> **"THESE SKILLS ARE A POWERFUL START THAT YOU CAN USE TO GET PAST YOUR INITIAL RELUCTANCE OR FEAR OF CONFLICT, TO TREAT IT LESS AS SOMETHING TO AVOID, AND MORE AS SOMETHING WE CAN RESOLVE TOGETHER.**

make others feel excluded or hurt, and refuse to change practices or processes that maintain inequity. Because we can't eliminate harm immediately (though we can try to reduce it), it's imperative that we're able to handle and address it when it happens. As for conflict? It's inevitable—and in many cases, even beneficial. But creating positive outcomes from harm or conflict takes skill.

The first and most simple skill might be the hardest: listening. Not listening immediately to judge or act, but listening simply to understand. Learning how to manage conflict, especially when working with parties that struggle to listen or work together, is the extension of this skill. Oftentimes, there's a less-obvious hidden root cause or causes undergirding conflict. Learning to recognize and diagnose this can guide our actions in repairing harm: recognizing the hurt that has happened, understanding the reasons behind it, and guiding those involved to a resolution where possible.

These approaches to conflict resolution are hard, partly because they're unfamiliar to many of us. The way many of us have been taught formally and informally to address conflict is always to assign a perpetrator and a victim, to connect accountability with punishment, and to treat conflict always as an interpersonal issue and never connected to larger systemic factors. But these approaches fail everyone involved, including those harmed. The skills in this section help outline a different path that avoids some of the common failures in conflict resolution: failing to listen to those impacted and imposing our own "solutions" onto problems that might not need them, failing to manage conflict and allowing it to escalate or devolve into something unmanageable over time, failing to identify the root cause behind conflict and thus seeing the same conflicts crop up again and again, and finally failing to resolve conflicts—resulting in broken relationships and damaged trust in each other and the organization.

There's a lot to be said about conflict resolution, far more than can fit in four exercises. But these skills are a powerful start that you can use to get past your initial reluctance or fear of conflict, to treat it less as something to avoid, and more as something we can resolve together.

25

Listen to Understand

Jumping to action, for many of us, is easier than stopping to listen. The question so many ask is, What do I do? It's a question that those of us who are practitioners are familiar with; the pressure to answer this question is constantly looming above us, especially if we enter situations full of conflict and misunderstanding. All of us have sped into action at some point, doing our best to solve problems we know little about while hoping our efforts work. The best practitioners and leaders, however, are able to pause, ground themselves, and just listen. Not necessarily to agree or disagree. Not necessarily to judge or take action immediately. Simply to understand, to take in multiple perspectives and consider them thoughtfully before choosing the course of action that's right.

Being able to listen, and to hold space for those we are listening to, is the basic building block of every form of conflict resolution. Listening tells people that we, on some fundamental level, believe that they matter and that their experiences are worth understanding.[37]

PRACTITIONER'S TIP

When we're under time pressure, a surprising side effect is that many of our relational skills simply short-circuit. If we're under pressure to end a conflict, we'll only "listen" with the intention to immediately take action. If we're under pressure to run to our next commitment, we'll only "listen" with the intention of ending the conversation as quickly as possible. Active listening starts with perhaps one of the hardest prerequisites of all: time carved aside explicitly to pause, listen, understand, and *nothing else*, undergirded by the recognition that only with an understanding of others and their experiences can we embed respect for them in our actions. This is especially true when those we listen to are experiencing negative emotions—including when these emotions are directed at us! Use this exercise to move beyond the relational brick walls that can come up when talking about conflict or harm, when you're looking for a refresher on how you might slow down, take stock, and listen to understand.

LEARNING GOALS

- Understand active listening in action, and the four types of active listening skills.
- Practice responding to a situation involving conflict or harm.
- Brainstorm ways you might incorporate more active listening into your day-to-day routine.

UNDERSTAND YOURSELF

EXPAND YOUR CAPACITY

RELY ON OTHERS

FIND YOUR PLACE

DIAGNOSE INEQUITY

CHAMPION INCLUSION

ADDRESS CONFLICT AND HARM

ORGANIZE A MOVEMENT

REIMAGINE SYSTEMS

ACHIEVE DEI

INSTRUCTIONS

Follow the examples in the chart on the opposite page to learn about the four types of active listening skills and see them in action. Then, fill in the empty boxes in the chart with your own example of a situation where you would be *responding to conflict or harm* (whether involving you or not) and how you might use each of the four types of skills in your responses. Finally, answer the reflection questions.

Active Listening in Action

Active listening is "active" because it is focused, voluntary, and intentional—rather than accidental, passive, involuntary, or effortless. It is listening for the purpose of both understanding and helping the other person feel listened to, and for this reason it is a key relational foundation of any effort to address conflict and harm. While every person has different preferences when it comes to what helps them feel listened to, for most people, reflecting or paraphrasing their message, asking thoughtful questions, verbal affirmation, and validating emotion are all useful ways to demonstrate active listening.[38] These skills can make or break the first crucial minutes of interaction after conflict or harm has occurred, and in general they will improve your ability to hold space for people, even in emotionally charged situations.

REFLECTION QUESTIONS

1. Which of these four skills, if any, do you use in your regular day-to-day interactions or otherwise feel easy to you?

_____

_____

_____

_____

2. Which of these four skills feels the most out of the ordinary, unusual, or challenging for you?

_____

_____

_____

_____

SKILL	DEFINITION	EXAMPLE OF SKILL IN ACTION	YOUR CONTEXT
Responding to Conflict or Harm		**A colleague tells you that an interaction between you two felt upsetting and frustrating.**	
Reflecting	Summarizing or restating the gist of the speaker's comment or story	"It sounds like you're saying that the way I engaged with you in the moment felt patronizing."	
Thoughtful questioning	Asking a question that demonstrates comprehension	"You mentioned that you've felt this way in the past too. Can I ask what patterns you've seen over time?"	
Verbal affirmation	Thanking the speaker for reaching out and talking with you	"I appreciate you sharing that with me. I'm glad you felt like you could come to me to talk about it."	
Validating emotion	Naming and explicitly affirming the emotion the speaker expressed	"It makes sense to feel upset and frustrated from that interaction. I'm sorry I hurt you."	

Sidebar: UNDERSTAND YOURSELF · EXPAND YOUR CAPACITY · RELY ON OTHERS · FIND YOUR PLACE · DIAGNOSE INEQUITY · CHAMPION INCLUSION · ADDRESS CONFLICT AND HARM · ORGANIZE A MOVEMENT · REIMAGINE SYSTEMS · ACHIEVE DEI

3. It can feel much more challenging to practice active listening in a situation where *you* were personally involved in conflict or harm, compared to a situation you're not involved in. Why might this be the case, and what does it feel like for you?

_____

_____

_____

_____

4. What are some situations in which it's difficult to practice active listening, and why?

_____

_____

_____

_____

5. In these situations, what might you do to stay grounded and maintain your commitment to practicing these skills?

_____

_____

_____

_____

6. With any skill, the more you practice it, the better you become at using it. How might you make more opportunities in your life to practice these four types of active listening? In what situations can you see it helping you?

_____

_____

_____

_____

NOTES

37. Boogaard, Kat. "Active Listening: Benefits, Techniques, and Examples." Work Life by Atlassian, May 10, 2023. https://www.atlassian.com/blog/communication/active-listening.

38. Lebow, Hilary I. "Become a Better Listener: Active Listening." Psych Central, September 28, 2021. https://psychcentral.com/lib/become-a-better-listener-active-listening.

" LISTENING TELLS PEOPLE THAT WE, ON SOME FUNDAMENTAL LEVEL, BELIEVE THAT THEY MATTER AND THAT THEIR EXPERIENCES ARE WORTH UNDERSTANDING.

26

Manage Conflict

Conflict will happen. Difference in beliefs, values, or opinions means that disagreement and conflict are normal parts of working together, but that need not even be a negative thing: conflict managed well has well-documented positive effects, including exposure to new ideas and improved ability to express our needs, and it leads to better problem-solving.

But just as conflict takes many forms, conflict can be managed in many ways. Some forms of conflict management tend to have negative associations, like conflict avoidance and resolving conflicts through authority, while others are typically thought of more positively, like collaborative, group-centered approaches to problem-solving. But all have their place, their strengths and weaknesses—and for leaders who are often operating in a range of contexts and with a range of constraints, becoming skilled is less about picking one "best" kind of style, and more about knowing when to use what conflict management style and why.

PRACTITIONER'S TIP

Nobody finds it natural to use every kind of conflict management style at first, and that's to be expected. The styles that come most intuitively to us are often based on our upbringing, our cultural identities, our life experiences, or even the conflict management styles of our organizations, and no two people are exactly the same. Think of a conflict management style like a "language": the more you're able to use it fluently, the more adept you will be in a variety of different situations, with a variety of different people. The ideal is to be able to switch "languages" on a dime to pick the conflict management style that most effectively meets our goals, and adjust our approach on the fly as situations change. Use this exercise to plan out the styles you might use to manage conflict in your own context.

LEARNING GOALS

- Learn about the five conflict management styles.[39]
- Brainstorm situations in which each conflict management style would be effective.
- Practice applying the five conflict management styles to conflicts that you might experience in your context.

UNDERSTAND YOURSELF

EXPAND YOUR CAPACITY

RELY ON OTHERS

FIND YOUR PLACE

DIAGNOSE INEQUITY

CHAMPION INCLUSION

ADDRESS CONFLICT AND HARM

ORGANIZE A MOVEMENT

REIMAGINE SYSTEMS

ACHIEVE DEI

INSTRUCTIONS

Read about the five conflict management styles and the contexts in which they're effective. For each, review the example and brainstorm a situation where that style might be effective. Then, answer the remaining exercise questions to come up with some common conflicts in your context and the conflict management styles that might effectively address them.

The Five Conflict Management Styles

AVOIDANCE

Conflict avoidance is when a leader withdraws from a conflict. They may expect others to resolve the conflict without them or hope that the conflict will disappear over time. This style of conflict management can be useful when issues are small or inconsequential, or if there are good odds that the conflict will subside over time. However, this style of conflict management may cause problems if the conflict requires leadership participation, if the issue is large or threatens to get larger over time, or if the issue is time bound.

ACCOMMODATION

Conflict accommodation is when a leader puts their needs aside to resolve the conflict by "keeping the peace" and accommodating the larger or more popular party. This style of conflict resolution can be useful when an issue is more important to one party than to the leader or other parties, when building social capital or goodwill through a more passive leadership style is valuable, and during moments of crisis when maintaining team harmony is important. However, if the outcome is critical to the success of the team or the leader is already being doubted for being a "pushover," using an accommodating style may sow doubts about the leader's abilities.

COMPETITION

Conflict competition is when a leader uses their power and influence to make a decision, potentially disregarding the opinions or desires of other parties. This style of conflict resolution is useful during crises when immediate decisions are needed, when a certain outcome cannot be compromised on, or when the well-being or survival of the group is at stake. But when relationships are strained, the outcomes are not important to the team or organization, or alternatives exist, using a competing style may break team trust, spawn further conflict or revolt, and damage leadership credibility.

COMPROMISE

Conflict compromise is when a leader seeks to find an acceptable but suboptimal middle ground between all parties. This style of conflict resolution is one of the fastest and easiest, and so can be useful when a temporary or quick decision is needed, all parties in the conflict possess similar levels of power, or compromise will have a symbolic value for the team or organization. However, if there are power imbalances between parties, a leader who frequently compromises may be taken advantage of by parties seeking to further their agenda by sustaining conflict.

COLLABORATION

Conflict collaboration is when a leader works closely with all parties to ensure that conflicts are resolved in a way that benefits everyone. This style of conflict resolution is time, energy, and resource intensive but has many positive impacts on team unity, creativity, and satisfaction. It's most useful when all parties' issues are too important to compromise, when long-standing interpersonal conflict needs resolving, and when a solution is not needed immediately. However, if there are limited resources or time pressure, or if the issues being addressed are less impactful for the group, this approach can bog down decision-making and lower efficacy.

1. Review the five conflict management styles and examples of them in action in the chart. For each, think of an example in your own context (a hypothetical example is fine) for a conflict that might be best managed by the style in question.

STYLE	DEFINITION	MORE EFFECTIVE WHEN	LESS EFFECTIVE WHEN
Avoidance	Ignoring or abdicating from conflict	▪ The underlying issue is small or inconsequential ▪ The conflict is likely to resolve over time without intervention	▪ The underlying issue is highly consequential, or could worsen ▪ The conflict requires leadership intervention to resolve

EXAMPLE

Two employees who share a desk are bickering about each other's cleanliness preferences and ask their manager to resolve the issue. The manager tells them that they are responsible for figuring it out themselves.

YOUR CONTEXT
What is a conflict that might be best managed by conflict avoidance?

UNDERSTAND YOURSELF

EXPAND YOUR CAPACITY

RELY ON OTHERS

FIND YOUR PLACE

DIAGNOSE INEQUITY

CHAMPION INCLUSION

ADDRESS CONFLICT AND HARM

ORGANIZE A MOVEMENT

REIMAGINE SYSTEMS

ACHIEVE DEI

STYLE	DEFINITION	MORE EFFECTIVE WHEN	LESS EFFECTIVE WHEN
Accommo-dation	Keeping the peace by deferring to the larger or popular party	■ The underlying issue is unimportant to most parties ■ Building goodwill or team harmony is valuable	■ The underlying issue is highly important to team functioning ■ The leader is already being seen as a "pushover" or weak leader

EXAMPLE

A group of women are pushing for the office thermostat to be set to the mid-70s Fahrenheit, while a group of men wants the temperature to be in the mid-60s. Office managers decide to make the office temperature 73 degrees, since the issue is highly important to the women but less important to the men, and this decision will build goodwill.

YOUR CONTEXT
What is a conflict that might be best managed by conflict accommodation?

STYLE	DEFINITION	MORE EFFECTIVE WHEN	LESS EFFECTIVE WHEN
Competition	Using authority to make a unilateral decision	■ There is a crisis requiring immediate decisions or with only one decision available ■ The well-being or survival of the group is at stake	■ The outcomes are not important to the group, or no known alternatives exist ■ Relationships between the group and leaders are strained

EXAMPLE

An internal initiative is leaked to the press, generating negative media attention and controversy, resulting in the board of directors demanding the initiative be pulled. Senior leaders dissolve the initiative for one financial year and begin working with initiative members afterwards to figure out an alternative.

YOUR CONTEXT
What is a conflict that might be best managed by conflict competition?

STYLE	DEFINITION	MORE EFFECTIVE WHEN	LESS EFFECTIVE WHEN
Compromise	Finding an acceptable but suboptimal middle ground	▪ A quick decision is needed, even if temporary ▪ All parties possess similar power, or compromise has symbolic value for the group	▪ There is little time pressure ▪ There are power imbalances between different groups involved ▪ Leaders frequently compromise

EXAMPLE

Existing employee resource groups are advocating against the formation of a new ERG due to funding being stretched between more groups. Senior leaders approve the formation of a new ERG, lowering the budget for all ERGs slightly and giving the new group an even smaller budget, with promises to revisit the funding process the following year.

YOUR CONTEXT
What is a conflict that might be best managed by conflict compromise?

STYLE	DEFINITION	MORE EFFECTIVE WHEN	LESS EFFECTIVE WHEN
Collaboration	Resolving conflicts in a way benefiting everyone by attending to all needs	▪ All parties' issues are too important to compromise ▪ Long-standing interpersonal conflict needs resolving ▪ There is little time pressure	▪ There are limited resources and high time pressure ▪ The outcomes being addressed are not important to the group

EXAMPLE

Significant and recurring conflict occurs every year between sales teams, the corporate social responsibility team, and senior leaders over how the organization reconciles corporate purpose with its sales strategies. With outside facilitation, all parties come together to redesign the following year's overall corporate strategy to align with everyone's needs.

YOUR CONTEXT
What is a conflict that might be best managed by conflict collaboration?

UNDERSTAND YOURSELF

EXPAND YOUR CAPACITY

RELY ON OTHERS

FIND YOUR PLACE

DIAGNOSE INEQUITY

CHAMPION INCLUSION

ADDRESS CONFLICT AND HARM

ORGANIZE A MOVEMENT

REIMAGINE SYSTEMS

ACHIEVE DEI

2. What are some common conflicts you experience or have experienced in your own organization or community? Brainstorm three and list them in the following boxes.

Conflict 1
Conflict 2
Conflict 3

3. What conflict management style would you utilize within each of these conflicts, and why?

Conflict 1
Conflict 2
Conflict 3

4. Which conflict management styles feel the most comfortable to use for you vs. the most difficult? How might you practice utilizing the styles you're less comfortable with?

NOTE

39. Herrity, Jennifer. "5 Major Conflict Management Styles for Successful Managers." Indeed Career Guide, March 10, 2023. https://www.indeed.com/career-advice/career-development/conflict-management.

" THINK OF A CONFLICT MANAGEMENT STYLE LIKE A 'LANGUAGE': THE MORE YOU'RE ABLE TO USE IT FLUENTLY, THE MORE ADEPT YOU WILL BE IN A VARIETY OF DIFFERENT SITUATIONS, WITH A VARIETY OF DIFFERENT PEOPLE.

27

Repair Harm

Conflict doesn't always result in harm, but when it does, it's critical that leaders know how to address and resolve it. The challenge is that the common approach to accountability is punitive: it seeks to assign blame and mete out punishment for rule-breaking behavior, and little more. But punitive approaches don't actually solve problems. They fracture communities, enforce compliance through fear, and don't even meet the needs of those harmed along the way. A more restorative process[40] asks different questions that center the needs of those harmed, and as a result it allows for harm to be repaired without destroying the communities harm occurs within.

Restorative processes put relationships first, and guide people to repairing the harm caused. If hurtful comments or biased behavior occur, restorative processes will center the needs of those harmed, to determine what's required to "make things right"—and often, the solution will involve harmers apologizing, making amends, and changing behavior rather than punitive action. Of course, not every incident can be solved with a restorative process. But adding these practices to your toolbox can only increase your ability as a practitioner to address harm when it occurs.

PRACTITIONER'S TIP

A common first reaction to learning about restorative approaches to harm is to try and make sweeping generalizations about the outcomes these approaches seek. But the difference between a restorative and a punitive approach to resolving harm is primarily in the *process*, not the solutions. Rather than some external third party trying to match a transgression to a punishment without feedback from the people harmed, in a restorative process the people harmed are in the driver's seat—and no two people will want the same kinds of resolutions. Resist the urge to make generalizations like "restorative processes are about making apologies" or "restorative processes are about talking it out." Instead, recognize that the focus is on a process that makes those involved in and affected by harm feel listened to, supported, and empowered. Use this exercise to remind yourself what harm repair in action can look like.

LEARNING GOALS

- Learn how to use a restorative process for incidents of harm.
- Reflect on experiences of being harmed and harming others.
- Practice going through a restorative process.

UNDERSTAND YOURSELF

EXPAND YOUR CAPACITY

RELY ON OTHERS

FIND YOUR PLACE

DIAGNOSE INEQUITY

CHAMPION INCLUSION

ADDRESS CONFLICT AND HARM

ORGANIZE A MOVEMENT

REIMAGINE SYSTEMS

ACHIEVE DEI

INSTRUCTIONS

Learn about basic restorative harm resolution practices from the following text. Afterwards, answer the exercise and reflection questions to apply these ideas in your own context.

Repairing Harm by Restoring Relationships

Every act of harm impacts people. Restorative practices center this fact and focus on the relationships that were damaged, rather than the rules that were broken, when harm occurred. They ask the questions, What relationships were damaged? Who was harmed, and in what way? What needs weren't met for those impacted? What are the obligations of those who harmed others to make things right? The answers to these questions help inform the impacted parties, often not just the harmer and the people directly harmed, but also members of the community and anyone else impacted by the harm, to decide how the relationships can be mended, harm repaired, and needs met.[41]

While more traditional consequences like disciplinary action or removal from an environment can emerge from a restorative process, they are the exception and not the rule, and often they are chosen by those impacted as severe consequences to match a severe degree of harm committed. What often emerges from a restorative process, however, is a much broader spectrum of restoration and accountability than simple removal or punishment. If the harm was slight, sometimes a simple apology is enough to repair the breach. If the harm was complex and involved many people, the resolution of it can be as complex and multiparty as it needs to be to make things right.

Using these processes informally and interpersonally within working environments requires little more than the skill to do so, along with the shared expectations among a team that they will first try to resolve issues within the community before turning to more formal (often punitive) organizational disciplinary processes.

1. Think of a time when you *experienced* harm from another person or people. It can be any example, from any point in your life. What happened, what harm occurred, and why?

----

2. What did you feel, during and after the situation, about yourself, the harmer, and the caused harm itself?

_____

_____

_____

_____

3. What did you need from others, especially the harmer, to feel like the harm was repaired and things were made right? If the harm wasn't made right, what _would_ you have needed?

_____

_____

_____

_____

4. Now, think of a time when _you harmed_ another person or people. It can be any example, from any point in your life. What happened, who was harmed, and why?

_____

_____

_____

_____

5. What did you feel, during and after the situation, about yourself, the person harmed, and the caused harm itself?

_____

_____

_____

_____

6. What did you need from others, especially the harmed, to feel like the harm was repaired and things were made right? If the harm wasn't made right, what was missing?

_____

_____

_____

_____

Now, imagine a new situation:

> Angela felt upset that a promotion she felt she deserved went to a newer employee who she helped train, Jonathan, and humiliated that now she had to report to him. While working on Jonathan's team for a project requested by the department head, who makes promotion decisions, Angela made an offhand remark during an important client meeting that made Jonathan look incompetent and that confused the client. Jonathan, angry, confronted Angela and called her a "liability to the team" during the next team meeting, which stunned the team.

You're a neutral third party working with Angela, Jonathan, the team, and department leadership to facilitate a process among all parties to repair the harm that occurred. Reflect on your answers to questions 1–6 as you work through the following questions.

7. For the people who caused harm, you want to help them understand the impact of their behaviors, take responsibility for their actions, and work to repair the harm. Who would you work with, and how would you engage with them?

_____

_____

_____

_____

8. For the people who were harmed, you want to help them feel supported and safe, empower them to articulate their own desires for how to repair the harm committed, and encourage them to express their needs for healing. Who would you work with, and how would you engage with them?

_____

_____

_____

_____

9. For all others impacted, you want to help them feel informed about the situation, encourage them to share their concerns, and involve them in the reintegration of people who caused harm. How might you create these outcomes?

----

10. In this situation, what might a final resolution look like in which harm is repaired?

----

11. This situation is complicated—like many in real life are—because there isn't any one clear "harmer" and one clear "harmed." Because there are many sources of harm and many people harmed, the resolution requires more effort and buy-in from all parties involved. If this situation occurred in a traditional "accountability" context, involving punishment and discipline, how do you imagine it might be "resolved"? What would the shortcomings of this "resolution" be?

REFLECTION QUESTIONS

1. What feelings are most common when you are harmed? Why might these feelings come up?

UNDERSTAND YOURSELF

EXPAND YOUR CAPACITY

RELY ON OTHERS

FIND YOUR PLACE

DIAGNOSE INEQUITY

CHAMPION INCLUSION

ADDRESS CONFLICT AND HARM

ORGANIZE A MOVEMENT

REIMAGINE SYSTEMS

ACHIEVE DEI

2. How does our society or organization typically respond to people who have been harmed? How does this response help or hurt their healing?

3. What feelings are most common for you when you cause harm? Why might these feelings come up?

4. How does our society or organization typically respond to people who have caused harm? How does this response help or hurt their healing?

5. What feels most novel or challenging about using this kind of restorative process as a facilitator or practitioner? How might we gain proficiency in using these skills?

6. What would it look like to use some version of a restorative process, even an informal one, in a team environment? What would have to happen for this to be successful?

NOTES

40. Steward, Heather. "Restorative Practices in the Workplace." Edited by Paula Drouin. ADR Learning Institute, October 29, 2019. https://adrlearninginstitute.ca/restorative-practices-in-the-workplace/.

41. Government of Canada, Department of Justice. "Restorative Justice." Department of Justice, December 10, 2021. https://www.justice.gc.ca/eng/cj-jp/rj-jr/index.html.

UNDERSTAND YOURSELF

EXPAND YOUR CAPACITY

RELY ON OTHERS

FIND YOUR PLACE

DIAGNOSE INEQUITY

CHAMPION INCLUSION

ADDRESS CONFLICT AND HARM

ORGANIZE A MOVEMENT

REIMAGINE SYSTEMS

ACHIEVE DEI

28

Unearth Root Causes

UNDERSTAND YOURSELF

EXPAND YOUR CAPACITY

RELY ON OTHERS

FIND YOUR PLACE

DIAGNOSE INEQUITY

CHAMPION INCLUSION

ADDRESS CONFLICT AND HARM

ORGANIZE A MOVEMENT

REIMAGINE SYSTEMS

ACHIEVE DEI

Restorative processes help us respond to harm when it occurs. But if the same kinds of harm keep occurring, as practitioners we need to go beyond addressing only one incident at a time to understand what is driving harm on a deeper level, so that we might reduce or even prevent harm from occurring in the first place. Doing so requires that we learn how to trace the symptoms of harm all the way back to their roots so that we may change them.

Where harm is individual and repairing harm is interpersonal, preventing future harm is systemic. Accordingly, to build skill in unearthing the root causes of harm, we have to draw on our ability to analyze systems and advocate for change, then connect the dots for those around us to build successful change-making movements. This final step is what turns a restorative process into a *transformative* one, not just for individual people, but for entire organizations.[42]

PRACTITIONER'S TIP

While those who commit harm should be held accountable, the root causes of harm are almost never in individual "bad people." Larger patterns of harm in an organization or community tell a different story about *bad systems* that drive individuals to inflict harm. If economic investment is disproportionately lower in a community, poverty will be more widespread, and crime rates higher. If someone's needs have been chronically unmet, but lashing out helps them feel validated, they will learn to lash out. As leaders we can't control every aspect of systemic inequity—but we can make sure that our organizations and workplaces aren't part of the problem. If harm is originating from broken policies, toxic cultures, poorly designed processes, or other things within the walls of an organization, we can target these root causes. Use this exercise to strategize on the root causes behind harm if you're starting to see a pattern and suspect something deeper.

LEARNING GOALS

- For an issue or incident of harm, diagnose the root causes of harm and their origins.
- Strategize about how you might change these root causes and the impact of doing so.

INSTRUCTIONS

Answer the exercise questions to fill in the following simple graphic with the *symptoms* of one experience of harm that you've faced or heard about in your organization, your analysis of the *problems* that cause those experiences of harm, and the root *causes* related to those problems.

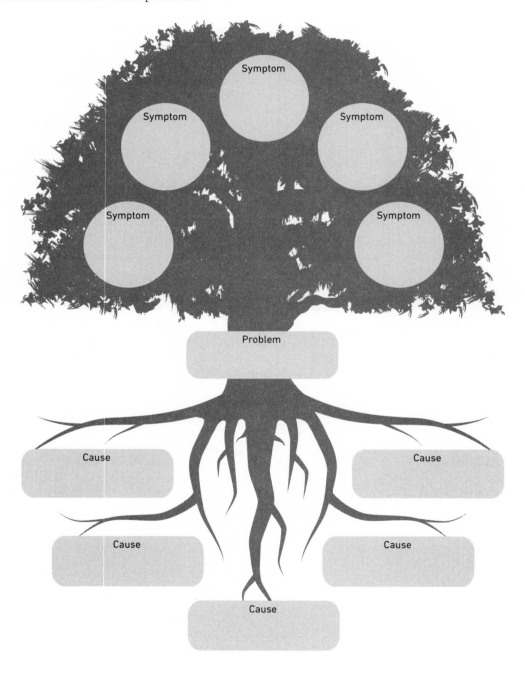

The Roots of DEI Problems

DEI practitioners often face many challenges in the role, challenges that can at first look unrelated. Tension every time senior leaders talk about DEI? Top-down pressure from the board of directors to diversify? A brain drain of skilled talent? The impulse is to treat them like unrelated problems to solve separately—the first with leadership communication training, the second with a DEI mission statement, and the third with more employee perks, for example. But if these solutions don't work, it might be because these challenges were more related than they appeared at first glance, as symptoms of a larger problem: slow progress on diversifying the representation of senior leadership, in this example.

If that slow progress results from a lack of succession planning, little accountability or incentive for senior leaders to change their behavior, low turnover, and an "old boy's club" mentality in which every leader seeks to protect the others, trying to use Band-Aid solutions focused on alleviating symptoms can only get us so far. We only change these patterns of harm by going beyond the symptoms of an issue to analyze their source, so that we might take effective action.

1. Name one complex and wide-reaching issue in your organization for this exercise. What makes it an issue?

_____

_____

_____

_____

2. What are some of the *downstream symptoms* of this issue? Think of the impact of this issue on your organization's people, policies, practices, and culture.

_____

_____

_____

_____

3. If you were to try and resolve these downstream symptoms individually, how would you do so? What would be the impact of these efforts?

_____

_____

_____

_____

UNDERSTAND YOURSELF

EXPAND YOUR CAPACITY

RELY ON OTHERS

FIND YOUR PLACE

DIAGNOSE INEQUITY

CHAMPION INCLUSION

ADDRESS CONFLICT AND HARM

ORGANIZE A MOVEMENT

REIMAGINE SYSTEMS

ACHIEVE DEI

4. Would most members of your organization agree that these downstream symptoms are tied to the issue you named? Why or why not?

_____

_____

_____

_____

5. What are the *root causes* of the issue? Draw on the following information about structure and culture if relevant in your answer.

STRUCTURE The set of rules, roles, and responsibilities that coordinate behavior and facilitate achieving the organization's goals		
CENTRALIZATION	FORMALIZATION	COMPLEXITY
The degree to which outcomes depend on controlled, powerful, top-down decisions	The degree to which formal rules, processes, and documentation govern behavior	The degree to which activities are split between people, jobs, roles, and locations

CULTURE The shared but unspoken values, assumptions, and expectations for behavior, embodied by rituals, stories, and beliefs			
POWER DISTANCE	INTERDEPENDENCE	UNCERTAINTY AVOIDANCE	FAILURE AVOIDANCE
The degree to which a large disparity between the most and least powerful is acceptable	The degree to which people perceive their outcomes as linked vs. separate	The degree to which people avoid, vs. embrace, uncertainty and ambiguity	The degree to which people avoid, vs. embrace, failure and imperfection

_____

_____

_____

_____

6. How would you address these root causes, what parties would you engage, and what actions would you take?

_____

_____

_____

_____

7. If you were successful in addressing these root causes, what impact would doing so have on the symptoms you named?

_____

_____

_____

_____

NOTE

42. Regan. "Transformative Justice." Project Respect, January 26, 2021. https://www.projectrespect .ca/2021/01/transformative-justice/.

UNDERSTAND YOURSELF

EXPAND YOUR CAPACITY

RELY ON OTHERS

FIND YOUR PLACE

DIAGNOSE INEQUITY

CHAMPION INCLUSION

ADDRESS CONFLICT AND HARM

ORGANIZE A MOVEMENT

REIMAGINE SYSTEMS

ACHIEVE DEI

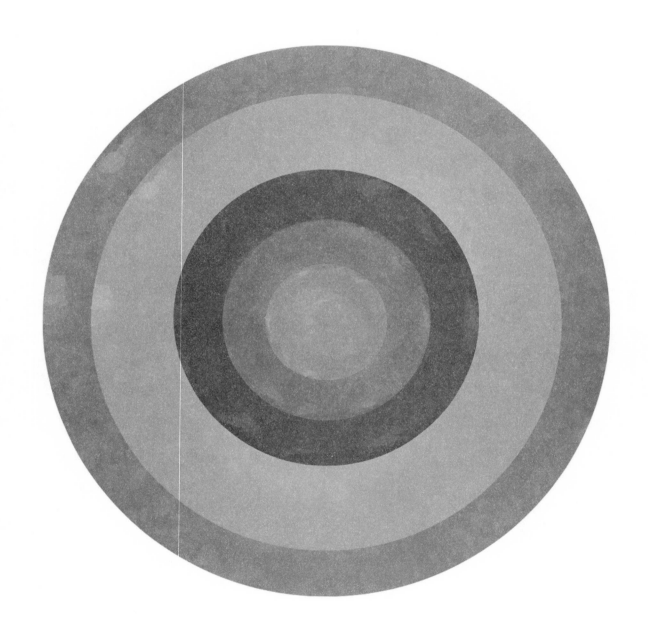

PART THREE

Achieve Outcomes

ORGANIZE A MOVEMENT

Every individual has the ability to create change, but no one individual has the ability to change a system on their own. Systems, institutions, structure, culture, and strategy are collectively created; for them to change, the effort to do so must be collective as well. But working collectively, even on challenges that are as important and pressing as DEI challenges, doesn't come naturally to many of us. The popular image of

> ❝ CHANGE IS HARD, NONLINEAR, AND TO SOME EXTENT, UNPREDICTABLE. BUT CONSISTENTLY, CHANGE TAKES MOVEMENTS.

change-making as the natural consequence of singular "heroes" drives many passionate practitioners to go at the work alone, and as a result fail on their own as well. Yet, the popular advice proliferates to find your voice, take the lead, and otherwise "leadership-self-help" your way to organizational change.

Practically every case study of successful organizational change speaks to the importance of movements, not just heroes. People coming together from all corners of the organization to build a better status quo. Fiery challenges from those who would burn the organization down out of a fervent belief that a far better version of it might rise from the ashes, met by institutionalists stewarding the organization's deep history and ethos. Messy change-making through coalitions, factions, networks, and grassroots movements at times working together and at times enmeshed in bitter conflict.

Any practitioner looking to create change must be able to roll their sleeves up and participate in these processes, casting aside the fantasy that some linear change management strategy espoused by an expensive consulting company will be able to do it all without a sweat. Change is hard, nonlinear, and to some extent, unpredictable. But consistently, change takes movements.

This section will teach practitioners how to engage effectively in basic movement-building work. Understanding and visualizing the strategies, agendas, and decisions of the many powerful groups and people in every organization helps us start thinking in the big picture. Mapping the power of these people can give us a sense of how they relate and may engage with our change-making movement. It also leads into coalition-building—how we attain the critical mass that all movements need by bringing together different parties willing to work together for a mutually beneficial cause.

To that end, the exercises in this section are more challenging and can be done in a group rather than only by individuals. They will push you to do the hard work of movement-building in practice and will teach you the building blocks to not only analyze movements, but create them yourselves.

Change-Making Roles in Action

What does it look like when we are able to work within movements to achieve change, rather than just on our own? Examples of successful movement work are illuminating, and there is one prominent example I have been involved in in which every movement role played a key part.

The movement started from the grassroots, as many do. A small group of employees with relatively little power got together to voice frustrations with their organization's anti-harassment training, cold and clinical mandatory sessions steeped in racial, gender, and sexuality-related stereotypes that were more likely to intimidate, scare, or even just bore the daylights out of attendees without meaningfully changing their behavior.

These were advocates, and they took their concerns to organizational leaders with a single, clear ask: "We need better trainings that focus more on positive, respectful, and inclusive behavior rather than using scare tactics to tell us what we *shouldn't* do." "We'll see what we can do," responded leaders, and that was the last of it that the advocates heard for a little while.

Behind the scenes, sympathetic leaders—backers—passed down the feedback, alongside other related messages they had heard from other employees and stakeholders sharing concerns from their teams, to the internal department that offered training: "Focus on positive behavior."

That department, at the time, was in the middle of a hiring search for a new director-level employee to improve on training programs and develop new ones. The leading candidates seemed largely cut from the same cloth as current employees, with the exception of a candidate with a unique background and skills in, miraculously, tackling difficult topics from a positivist and empowering lens. The directive couldn't have come at a better time, and the decision was suddenly far easier: the unique candidate was hired. The ball had started rolling.

Months after their meeting with organizational leaders, many of the advocates who had originally shared feedback received an email from a director they weren't familiar with, with a simple ask: "Can we chat about harassment training?" The earnestness of the email, coupled with the promise that this new leader would be less beholden to the machine of organizational politics, prompted many advocates to say yes. During the meeting, the new director spent a small amount of time asking questions, and the rest of the time listening, nodding, and furiously scribbling down notes. They asked about all the ways in which the current programs failed, and about employees' vision and ideas for a better replacement.

Weeks later, folks received a triumphant email. "We've received approval to add a new program to our new employee orientation," it read. "We're looking for helpers, and thought of you first."

The new director had been tirelessly working with leaders across the organization, especially longtime employees—strategists—who encouraged them to look into HR programs and employee processes. The new employee orientation was a powerful medium, though it was notoriously difficult to change. The director spent weeks identifying and speaking to important

> **WHEN PEOPLE ACROSS ORGANIZATIONS ALL PLAY THEIR ROLES EFFECTIVELY AT THE RIGHT PLACE AND TIME—THE TYPE OF RADICAL CHANGE THAT TRANSFORMS AN ORGANIZATION IS VERY MUCH POSSIBLE.**

allies—backers—about their vision for the event and ultimately *succeeded* in getting approval from the decision-makers who controlled the coveted orientation program. As the director started working with builders to create this program and make it effective in the context of the new employee orientation, they began reaching out to advocates to update them on the progress that had been made, and for help building out the program's content.

Because of the trust that had been built, the advocates said yes. They worked with builders to ensure that it not only took a more positive spin on anti-harassment, but also avoided many of the problematic pitfalls of the old program. One of the many additions to the program they implemented included, for example, coordinating and resourcing managers of new employees to follow up on the program with continued conversations on their wider teams. After months, happy with what felt genuinely like a radically new and effective program, advocates began tapping their networks for peers to volunteer as participants in the program and to promote it as educators and organizers. Some wrote articles shared on the company intranet describing their excitement that such a program was happening. Others encouraged their managers to attend as spectators, in the hopes that they would be open to similar conversations with their existing teams, new employees or not. There were skeptics and detractors, of course—some employees openly scoffed about the program and doubted that it would be anything other than a waste of time. "Wait and see" was the response from organizers and educators.

The first iteration of the program, months later, was an unprecedented success. Interest in the program skyrocketed beyond expectations, thanks to the work of organizers and educators, and the director was flooded with interest from all corners of the organization. "It's not fair that only new employees receive this training," people said. "Can we attend too?"

And the movement took off. Strategists recommended expanding the program out to different cohorts in the organization's history, given their shared experiences, and creating new channels and groups to prepare for each year's new cohorts. Builders helped create these new programs and groups, and reformers tinkered with the original program, based on feedback from advocates and other stakeholders. Educators helped design resources for all managers to support conversations on this program, organizers rallied audiences to attend and participate, and backers worked to institutionalize it as an integral part of the organization's DNA.

When I checked back in on the program, years after its inception, I couldn't believe how normalized the once-radical idea had become. Conversations about inclusive behavior were the norm throughout the year. Leaders looked

forward to each year's cohort and the insights that would come from the program and its many spin-offs and follow-ups. Years of constant refinement and improvement had produced a self-sustaining and effective program that had embedded itself into the fabric of the organization's culture and structure—a resounding success.

I share this story to highlight that when the stars align—when people across organizations all play their roles effectively at the right place and time—the type of radical change that transforms an organization is very much possible. If we strive intentionally and critically, it can be possible for our organizations too.

" EVERY INDIVIDUAL
HAS THE ABILITY TO
CREATE CHANGE,
BUT NO ONE INDIVIDUAL
HAS THE ABILITY TO
TO CHANGE A SYSTEM
ON THEIR OWN.

29

Scout Your Movement

You can't build a movement until you understand everything there is to know about the issue it will address front to back, including everyone it affects, because these are the people who will be active members within your movement, be potential backers of it, or work to oppose it. Oftentimes, this work of research and fact-finding will reveal surprises: like already-existing efforts to create the change you're hoping for, or valuable information on how past efforts to address the issue have failed.

Our goal is to ensure that a movement to address this issue is truly needed and, if it is, to gain as much information as possible to set it up for success. While it may feel easier to simply let your movement start "organically," you'll quickly hit walls that would have been easily avoided had you taken the time to research from the beginning. Scouting out your issue takes time, but before a movement starts, you have all the time in the world. The better prepared you are beforehand, the more likely it is that your movement finds success.

PRACTITIONER'S TIP

No one person will fully understand any issue, only their unique perspective on it. But this means that if you ask only one person about what the issue is and why it needs addressing, you'll receive by definition a biased answer. That includes *you*—and it's quite possible that even if you've done every exercise in this book up until this point, you've still got an incomplete understanding of the issue you want to solve. This is normal! The more you can approach the process of scouting your movement with an open mind, the more you'll learn and the more prepared you'll be to create a movement if needed. Use this exercise to structure your information-gathering process as you engage with other people and groups.

LEARNING GOALS

- Brainstorm a list of relevant parties that have something to gain or lose from a potential movement around a DEI issue, or power to affect it.[43]
- Gather information to research the priorities and needs of these important parties.

INSTRUCTIONS

Answer the exercise questions to strategize about people and groups most relevant to a movement. Then, fill in the chart with information that you've learned about these parties. Afterwards, answer the reflection questions.

1. Choose one DEI-related issue or initiative to focus on, throughout Exercises 29–32, that you believe requires a movement to address. It does not need to be one you've taken any steps to address or gathered data for. Name your issue or initiative below.

_____

_____

_____

_____

2. Name *as many relevant parties in your context as you can think of* that might have something to gain or lose from a movement around the issue you chose. They can be individuals, informal and formal groups, or any other party. Focus on quantity and not quality at this stage.

_____

_____

_____

_____

_____

3. From this list, pick three relevant parties that might have *the most to gain*, and three that might have *the most to lose* from a movement. If you can't name three from each category, go back to the previous step to brainstorm more. List them here.

SOMETHING TO GAIN	SOMETHING TO LOSE
1.	1.
2.	2.
3.	3.

From the same list, pick three relevant parties that might have *the most influence* over the outcomes the movement is trying to create, regardless of whether they have something to lose or gain. List them here. You can list parties more than once if they appear in other lists.

MOST INFLUENCE
1.
2.
3.

4. Now, choose *four* of the parties you named, to actually research. You can ask questions of them directly, speak with those who know them well, make inferences from your own experiences with them, or all of the above. To guide your thinking, follow the prompts to fill in the chart with information about each party you've researched. If you're not able to provide the information with confidence, use your best guess but challenge yourself to seek that information out before moving forward if possible. Afterwards, answer the reflection questions.

RELEVANT PARTY Who are you researching?	GAIN/LOSE If a movement occurred, how would they benefit or lose from it?	PRIORITIES, AGENDA, POWER What are their own goals and priorities, and how would a movement fit?
VP of Marketing Joanne	In a movement to end informal hiring, Joanne's team would struggle. They've relied heavily on informal processes to hire their friends. Joanne would lose team support if she supported this effort.	Joanne wants her team to have faith that even if the organization changes, the team will not. However, she also doesn't want to look like a selfish VP to her peers. A movement will introduce tension to these competing goals.

CONTINUED ▶

UNDERSTAND YOURSELF

EXPAND YOUR CAPACITY

RELY ON OTHERS

FIND YOUR PLACE

DIAGNOSE INEQUITY

CHAMPION INCLUSION

ADDRESS CONFLICT AND HARM

ORGANIZE A MOVEMENT

REIMAGINE SYSTEMS

ACHIEVE DEI

RELEVANT PARTY Who are you researching?	GAIN/LOSE If a movement occurred, how would they benefit or lose from it?	PRIORITIES, AGENDA, POWER What are their own goals and priorities, and how would a movement fit?

REFLECTION QUESTIONS

1. Many people find it easier to brainstorm people who have something to gain from a movement than people who have something to lose from it. What was your experience? Did you have to go back to think of more people or groups?

_____

_____

_____

_____

2. What was your experience selecting relevant parties to your potential movement from the larger list that you were able to brainstorm? How did you eventually narrow down your list?

_____

_____

_____

_____

3. Scouting out an issue almost always requires doing additional research to learn things we weren't aware of when we first started thinking about the issue. What additional research did you do, if any, and what was most interesting or surprising about what you found out?

_____

_____

_____

_____

4. Now that you've completed the chart, what next steps come to mind? How might you use this valuable information you compiled to plan out a successful movement?

_____

_____

_____

_____

NOTE

43. Panorama Consulting Group. "The Role of a Stakeholder Analysis in Change Management [4 Reasons It's Essential]." Panorama Consulting Group, August 10, 2022. https://www.panorama -consulting.com/stakeholder-analysis-in-change-management/.

UNDERSTAND YOURSELF

EXPAND YOUR CAPACITY

RELY ON OTHERS

FIND YOUR PLACE

DIAGNOSE INEQUITY

CHAMPION INCLUSION

ADDRESS CONFLICT AND HARM

ORGANIZE A MOVEMENT

REIMAGINE SYSTEMS

ACHIEVE DEI

30

Map
Power

Not every constituent or interest group has the same access to power, which makes thinking about power critically and thoughtfully a prerequisite to organizing effective movements. Targeting people with less power may make it easier to find allies, but it might make it challenging to reach those who control the systems we're trying to change. Targeting people with more power may keep us focused on our goals, but it might make it challenging to build the critical mass needed for any movement to gain relevance.

Mapping out the power that different people and groups related to a particular issue have access to can inform a movement's tactics and strategy, and identify gaps in engagement that, left unaddressed, leave movements vulnerable.[44] It's a skill that not only helps practitioners and leaders start movements, but also sustains them over time even as the organizational landscape and the players on it change.

PRACTITIONER'S TIP

Be careful not to let your assumptions about power compromise the process of genuinely learning about how it manifests. Sure, on average the most senior leader with the longest tenure and the most privileged social identities might have the most power, and the most junior employee with the shortest tenure and most marginalized social identities might have the least—but is that the case for *your* organization, and the people within it? How can you be sure, unless you put aside your preconceived ideas and seek to find out? What you will likely find is that your hunches will be mostly right, but with some surprising and game-changing exceptions. You might find that someone who fits the profile of an opponent to your movement has great reasons for supporting it, or that someone who you saw as a staunch ally might in fact be dead set against helping. Use this exercise to build on what you know about potential movement allies and opponents, to plan out your movement strategy.

LEARNING GOALS

- Analyze people and groups to create unique power profiles.
- Visualize stakeholder power and make connections to movement strategy.

UNDERSTAND YOURSELF

EXPAND YOUR CAPACITY

RELY ON OTHERS

FIND YOUR PLACE

DIAGNOSE INEQUITY

CHAMPION INCLUSION

ADDRESS CONFLICT AND HARM

ORGANIZE A MOVEMENT

REIMAGINE SYSTEMS

ACHIEVE DEI

INSTRUCTIONS

Follow the exercise questions to analyze the power of four different parties relevant to your movement, and visualize your analysis on "hard" and "soft" power maps. Afterwards, answer the reflection questions.

1. Review the types of power and the new organizational framework of "hard" vs. "soft" power.

HARD POWER	
Formal	The right or authority to request behavior from another
Reward	The ability to promise compensation to influence behavior
Coercive	The ability to threaten punishment to influence behavior
SOFT POWER	
Expert	The ability to influence behavior by being seen as possessing greater expertise
Information	The ability to influence behavior by possessing greater information
Referent	The ability to build rapport and influence behavior through charisma

2. Identify four parties relevant to your movement within your organization or community, and write their names on the chart. Next to each party, check the boxes corresponding to the types of power they have access to. Then describe their stance on your movement.

PERSON OR GROUP	HARD POWER			SOFT POWER		
	FORMAL	REWARD	COERCIVE	EXPERT	INFO	REFERENT
Joanne, VP marketing	✓	✓	✓			✓
STANCE:	Against, due to her strong relationship with a team that opposes movement goals because they stand to lose more than gain					
STANCE:						
STANCE:						
STANCE:						
STANCE:						

3. For each of the four people or groups, count the number of check marks they have in the *Hard Power* categories. Indicate each on the map according to the amount of power they have (if three checks then *High Power*, if two then *Medium Power*, if one or zero then *Low Power*) and their stance on your movement, from *Strongly Oppose* to *Strongly Support*.

HARD POWER MAP

High Power		High Power
Medium Power		Medium Power
Low Power		Low Power

Strongly Oppose   Oppose   Neutral   Support   Strongly Support

UNDERSTAND YOURSELF

EXPAND YOUR CAPACITY

RELY ON OTHERS

FIND YOUR PLACE

DIAGNOSE INEQUITY

CHAMPION INCLUSION

ADDRESS CONFLICT AND HARM

ORGANIZE A MOVEMENT

REIMAGINE SYSTEMS

ACHIEVE DEI

4. For each of the four people or groups, count the number of check marks they have in the *Soft Power* categories. Indicate each on the map according to the amount of power they have (if three checks then *High Power*, if two then *Medium Power*, and if one or zero then *Low Power*) and their stance on your movement, from *Strongly Oppose* to *Strongly Support*.

SOFT POWER MAP

High Power   High Power

Medium Power   Medium Power

Low Power   Low Power

Strongly   Strongly
Oppose   Oppose   Neutral   Support   Support

REFLECTION QUESTIONS

1. Look back over the power you attributed to the four people or groups you identified as relevant to your movement. How do these different parties differ in terms of power? Are there any dimensions of power that are over- or under-represented?

2. How does the *Hard Power* map compare to the *Soft Power* map? Where do you think these similarities and differences originate from, and what are the repercussions of this?

3. Following this exercise, how might you actually engage with the four people or groups you mapped out, to *mitigate or lessen their opposition*, or to *leverage or increase their support*?

4. Having filled out this chart and this graphic, what next steps come to mind? How might you use this valuable information you compiled to plan out a successful movement?

NOTE

44. Tang, Anita. "Power Mapping and Analysis." The Commons Social Change Library, April 20, 2023. https://commonslibrary.org/guide-power-mapping-and-analysis/.

UNDERSTAND YOURSELF

EXPAND YOUR CAPACITY

RELY ON OTHERS

FIND YOUR PLACE

DIAGNOSE INEQUITY

CHAMPION INCLUSION

ADDRESS CONFLICT AND HARM

ORGANIZE A MOVEMENT

REIMAGINE SYSTEMS

ACHIEVE DEI

31

Form a Coalition

People who start movements often hit a wall when they realize that while the first few supporters of a movement may come quickly, other powerful groups needed for a movement to take off are less easily brought on. Even those amenable to the effort often have their own agendas and needs that don't align perfectly with movement leaders'. In some cases, some of their agendas may even be outright oppositional. In these situations, to attain critical mass, many movements have to allow themselves to evolve—enough to bring in other parties and leverage their power, but not so much that the original goals of the movement are lost or co-opted.

This complex work of coalition-building is hard to learn through any other way besides direct experience. But one strategy you can start with is to draw creative connections between the agendas of the powerful parties you hope to work with and the "why" behind your movement.

PRACTITIONER'S TIP

Coalition-building isn't neat or clean. Coalitions are messy, emergent, and irrational, without formal structure, and they come about in the same way—often because different people and groups have their own reasons for working together on a shared goal.[45] Some coalition members participate because they want prestige or approval. Others do so because they would do anything in pursuit of "doing the right thing." Most get involved because there's something they stand to gain. For practitioners, this reality can be hard to swallow, because in an ideal world, everyone would participate in DEI work out of a sense of shared responsibility, and a shared belief in justice. To engage successfully in coalition-building, you have to ground yourself in the outcomes you hope to create, but let go of the idea that your movement will stay exactly the way it started. Use this exercise before you reach out to recruit others into a shared DEI movement.

LEARNING GOALS

- Learn how to analyze movement goals from multiple perspectives.
- Consider how you would use these perspectives to attract new partners in a coalition.
- Reflect on how you might need to adjust your original vision to expand your coalition.

UNDERSTAND YOURSELF

EXPAND YOUR CAPACITY

RELY ON OTHERS

FIND YOUR PLACE

DIAGNOSE INEQUITY

CHAMPION INCLUSION

ADDRESS CONFLICT AND HARM

ORGANIZE A MOVEMENT

REIMAGINE SYSTEMS

ACHIEVE DEI

INSTRUCTIONS

For a movement to address a DEI issue, follow the instructions to name and analyze movement goals and identify the needs of powerful people and groups with the potential to join a coalition. Then, answer the reflection questions.

Name Your Movement:

1. For your movement, share your "standard" answer to the question, Why, and how, should people take action? Draw on your knowledge of your organization, and discuss the benefits of your solutions to the groups most affected by inequity.

2. Name a powerful person or group that you might want as a key supporter of your movement but that may not be fully convinced by your standard rationale alone. Why not?

3. What are some nonobvious ways your movement might benefit them? What changes might you make to your movement to increase the overlap between your goals and theirs?

4. Use your answers to question 3 to create a tailored outreach message. In your answer, discuss how the action you want them to take would benefit your movement, and highlight how your movement would help them achieve their broader goals.

----

5. Now, name a powerful person or group who may be antagonistic or hostile, given your standard rationale, but might be neutral to your movement or even supportive.

----

6. What are some ways your movement might *not harm* or might even *benefit* them? What changes might you make to your movement to decrease the clash between your goals and theirs?

----

7. Use your answers to question 6 to create a tailored outreach message. In your answer, highlight the lack of harm (or the benefits) of your movement to their broader goals, and if relevant, offer them a way to get involved in the movement.

UNDERSTAND YOURSELF

EXPAND YOUR CAPACITY

RELY ON OTHERS

FIND YOUR PLACE

DIAGNOSE INEQUITY

CHAMPION INCLUSION

ADDRESS CONFLICT AND HARM

ORGANIZE A MOVEMENT

REIMAGINE SYSTEMS

ACHIEVE DEI

REFLECTION QUESTIONS

1. Compromising or adjusting our original "pure" vision or story for our movement in order to bring in other parties for a coalition, especially parties that might be antagonistic or hostile to our movement, often brings a high level of tension to movement-building. How might you navigate this kind of conflict in a way that feels authentic to yourself and your approach as a practitioner?

2. What was the biggest difference when modifying your movement's vision or goals for a potential key supporter vs. a potential antagonist or opponent? How did you approach the two different tasks?

3. Assuming there are many people or groups you might want in your coalition, all of whom may require slightly different approaches or stories to build buy-in, where will you draw your boundary for how far you're willing to modify or reframe your original argument for change?

4. As movements evolve in the process of building coalitions, they often gain complexity. How might you manage the complexity of your movement (potentially leveraging members of the coalition you're building) the way it ended up by the end of this exercise, compared to how it started off?

_____

_____

_____

_____

NOTE

45. Rodgers, Chris. _Informal Coalitions: Mastering the Hidden Dynamics of Organizational Change._ Palgrave Macmillan, 2007.

UNDERSTAND YOURSELF

EXPAND YOUR CAPACITY

RELY ON OTHERS

FIND YOUR PLACE

DIAGNOSE INEQUITY

CHAMPION INCLUSION

ADDRESS CONFLICT AND HARM

ORGANIZE A MOVEMENT

REIMAGINE SYSTEMS

ACHIEVE DEI

32

Bring People Together

The final step to get a movement off the ground is to put everything together. You scout your issue, identifying the people and groups most relevant to your movement's success. You map their access to power, identify those who might participate in your movement through a coalition, and secure their participation in your movement. All that's left is the hard part: bringing people together to play their unique roles in a successful movement. When everyone understands the part they have to play and how their role relates to others', movements gain the ability to create substantial, sustainable impact.

These roles—advocate, educator, organizer, strategist, backer, builder, and reformer—are not optional: if even one goes unfilled, movements run the risk of failure. And while people can play more than one role in a movement, a successful movement has many people playing each. Coalitions are critical simply to have the range of skills and resources needed for success.

PRACTITIONER'S TIP

Coalitions inherently involve conflict and disagreement. Members may disagree about ideology, approach, tactics, and even the end goals of the movement. This conflict is normal, and surprisingly, these questions don't have to be 100% resolved for coalitions to work successfully together. What may happen, however, is that different parties cycle in and out of coalitions at different points in time as their goals and capacity align or not with those of the movement. In poorly planned coalitions, this movement can mean the end of the entire movement, especially if one of the parties that leaves was one of the founding ones. But if we can plan out movement roles and bake in *redundancy*—the idea that no one role depends solely on one person, and that there are always backups—our movements will be able to survive these normal fluctuations.[46] Use this exercise to assign people within your movement to these roles.

LEARNING GOALS

- Chart how different people and groups in a coalition might participate in a DEI movement.
- Think about how to engage different people in their movement roles.

UNDERSTAND YOURSELF

EXPAND YOUR CAPACITY

RELY ON OTHERS

FIND YOUR PLACE

DIAGNOSE INEQUITY

CHAMPION INCLUSION

ADDRESS CONFLICT AND HARM

ORGANIZE A MOVEMENT

REIMAGINE SYSTEMS

ACHIEVE DEI

INSTRUCTIONS

Review the seven main movement roles. In the chart, list the major participants in your movement. For each, check the box for what movement role(s) they might play effectively, describe their role(s) in action, and suggest an engagement strategy. Afterwards, answer the reflection questions.

SEVEN MAIN MOVEMENT ROLES	
Advocate	Break the ice, raise awareness of issues, and add momentum to movements
Educator	Upskill and inform stakeholders at all stages in their learning journeys
Organizer	Attain a critical mass of stakeholders to achieve specific objectives
Strategist	Share a big picture perspective and facilitate movement direction and decisions
Backer	Formally and informally resource, support, and add legitimacy to movements
Builder	Create new policies, processes, and practices to implement new ideas
Reformer	Shape existing policies, processes, and practices to implement new ideas

1. For this exercise, brainstorm *five* members of your movement, in addition to yourself, who you think can collectively fill all seven movement roles. List these five members here.

1.	2.	3.	4.	5.

2. Fill in the chart with these five members and yourself, and for each, answer the prompts to strategize about their role(s) in action and how you might engage them in a movement. A sample answer is provided.

PARTICIPANT Who is this member?	MOVEMENT ROLES What movement roles do they fill?		THEIR ROLE(S) IN ACTION What actions would they take to fill these roles?	ENGAGEMENT STRATEGY How would the movement stay engaged with them?
The LGBTQ+ employee resource group	Advocate	✓	They would organize events to educate colleagues about the necessity of a new learning and development program from the angle of learning about LGBTQ+ identities and would make pilots or mock-up workshops to demonstrate the value of a dedicated program.	Include them in regular organizing meetings, and widely distribute the pilots and mock-up workshops to show the value of the learning and development program. Consult with them to make sure that movement language is inclusive of their members and constituents.
	Educator	✓		
	Organizer			
	Strategist			
	Backer			
	Builder	✓		
	Reformer			

PARTICIPANT	MOVEMENT ROLES		THEIR ROLE(S) IN ACTION	OUTREACH STRATEGY
You and/or your group	Advocate			
	Educator			
	Organizer			
	Strategist			
	Backer			
	Builder			
	Reformer			
	Advocate			
	Educator			
	Organizer			
	Strategist			
	Backer			
	Builder			
	Reformer			
	Advocate			
	Educator			
	Organizer			
	Strategist			
	Backer			
	Builder			
	Reformer			

CONTINUED ▶

UNDERSTAND YOURSELF

EXPAND YOUR CAPACITY

RELY ON OTHERS

FIND YOUR PLACE

DIAGNOSE INEQUITY

CHAMPION INCLUSION

ADDRESS CONFLICT AND HARM

ORGANIZE A MOVEMENT

REIMAGINE SYSTEMS

ACHIEVE DEI

PARTICIPANT	MOVEMENT ROLES		THEIR ROLE(S) IN ACTION	OUTREACH STRATEGY
	Advocate			
	Educator			
	Organizer			
	Strategist			
	Backer			
	Builder			
	Reformer			
	Advocate			
	Educator			
	Organizer			
	Strategist			
	Backer			
	Builder			
	Reformer			
	Advocate			
	Educator			
	Organizer			
	Strategist			
	Backer			
	Builder			
	Reformer			

REFLECTION QUESTIONS

1. Were the participants you selected able to cover all the movement roles at least once, and ideally twice for redundancy? If so, how did you achieve this? If not, what movement roles and participants are you missing?

2. What was your experience assigning effective movement roles to the participants you selected? What roles felt easier vs. harder to assign with confidence?

3. Which participants were most challenging to describe their role in action for? Why?

4. An engagement strategy helps us ensure that movement participants feel like the movement will benefit them, and like they are valuable to the movement. What was most challenging or surprising about coming up with engagement strategies for the participants you listed?

5. How do you envision the different roles in your movement working together once all roles have been filled? What might the arc of a successful movement using these participants look like?

NOTE

46. D'Alisa, Giacomo, Francesca Forno, and Simon Maurano. "Grassroots (economic) activism in times of crisis: Mapping the redundancy of collective actions." *Partecipazione e conflitto* 8, no. 2 (2015): 328–342.

" WHEN EVERYONE UNDERSTANDS THE PART THEY HAVE TO PLAY AND HOW THEIR ROLE RELATES TO THOSE OF OTHERS, MOVEMENTS GAIN THE ABILITY TO CREATE SUBSTANTIAL, SUSTAINABLE IMPACT.

REIMAGINE SYSTEMS

Systems change, even with a movement on your side, isn't easy. So many people that build and inherit organizations don't start off with a strong awareness of how their assumptions and behaviors might be biased, nor how these biases manifest in the world around them. And as a result, the organizations they build end up with systems that reinforce homogeneity, inequity, and exclusion, rather than diversity, equity, and inclusion. Changing systems that are entrenched in this way is like righting a house that's leaning: it'll require resetting the foundation (not just a cosmetic adjustment) and will take a proportionate amount of resources to do so—but it's quite possible.

> ❝ CREATING CHANGE AT SCALE REQUIRES UNDERSTANDING AND LEVERAGING THE TRUST, PATIENCE, AND GOODWILL OF YOUR WORKFORCE.

Movements are some of the most powerful tools practitioners can utilize and take part in to achieve these outcomes, but systems change isn't as easy as creating a movement and letting the rest happen organically. To begin with, creating change at scale requires understanding and leveraging the trust, patience, and goodwill of your workforce. And, to the great disappointment of practitioners looking for easy solutions, there's no ready-made formula to ensure change happens, only

thoughtful experiments targeting the underlying factors behind inequity, built on top of strong relationships with your customers. But one of the fundamental assumptions behind an approach that depends on experiments is that we can't assume that every experiment will succeed. Rigorous measurement helps us gauge progress and hold ourselves accountable. And understanding this progress in relation to our larger goals and objectives—the same that we grounded our efforts in to begin with— helps give us perspective on the systems change we've been able to create.

If we skip the step of understanding the trust we're working with in our organization, we'll run the risk of writing checks that bounce, deploying initiatives without the conditions necessary for them to succeed. If we copy and paste initiatives from listicles online into our own change-making efforts and promise others that these "best practices" are a guarantee for success, we'll be making promises we can't keep and setting ourselves up for embarrassing failures. In the DEI space, "systems change" is often framed as a thrilling but abstract endeavor. In actuality, successful systems change is almost entirely the opposite: a largely grounded, behind-the-scenes, and even occasionally bureaucratic process—punctuated with moments of action and dynamism—that's characterized by steady, collective efforts to achieve concrete wins over time.

Systemic Change in Action

You've just finished analyzing the data from an organization-wide survey, and one of your findings is clear: applicants with identities like "man" or "White" are advantaged over applicants with identities like "woman" or "Black" or "Latino" in the hiring process, all else equal. It can be tempting to look up "how to address hiring discrimination," identify the first intervention you find, like "deliver a bias training to your hiring managers," and eagerly deploy it with high hopes and little accountability.

I cannot stress this enough: taking this approach will jeopardize even the most carefully planned change-making movement. Do this, and you will fail dramatically and expensively. Throwing the first plausible intervention you find at a DEI problem is like hearing someone shout for help outside your window and throwing a fire extinguisher in the direction of their voice. It's sloppy and ineffective and, most importantly, might not solve any real problem to begin with.

Instead, when you know an outcome isn't what you want, you need to get deeply curious about the chain of events that causes it. Let's look at that hiring situation again and ask some questions. How do people come by your job postings? What factors do they consider, whether personal factors or aspects of the listing itself, before they decide to apply? How do candidates' applications themselves differ? Who are all the people within an organization involved in a hiring decision? What are all their roles in the process, and what factors do they consider about the candidate when they make decisions? How do they engage with candidates? How do interviews or skills tests feel to the candidates who take them? In general, when candidates "fall off" of the hiring process, where and why does it happen?

> **" YOU WON'T BE ABLE TO ACHIEVE DEI UNTIL YOU MOVE BEYOND A SIMPLISTIC VIEW OF 'BEST PRACTICES' AS YOUR DEFAULT ANSWER TO DEI CHALLENGES.**

Thoughtful change-makers, especially the decision-making backers and the strategists informing them, can find creative ways to ask and answer these questions. An applicant tracking system (ATS), for example, might already offer some insights into what stage of the process some candidates are eliminated in more than others.[47] Let's say that it's the first interview—women and men might apply and make it to the interview stage at similar rates, but from this point onwards women are disproportionately screened out. Why?

Post-interview surveys or one-on-ones sent out to all candidates might help you collect additional quantitative data. Of course, since you can't require all candidates to participate in this additional data collection process, you can't rule out response bias from which candidates might tend to answer a follow-up request from you. Nevertheless, you collect this data and analyze it alongside your existing demographic and organizational data, and in doing so you find something interesting: women candidates who interview with hiring managers working in a specific department, say marketing, are more likely to be rejected.

After interviewing a few people in marketing, you're able to develop a tentative theory about why. Perhaps the department was led by a longtime employee of the organization who was influential in leading his department and others through a crisis many years ago. His command-and-control leadership style was largely embraced by his department, with many modeling their work and communication style off of him. That leader had a particular talking point that he made over and over again: marketing, and the entire organization, was a place in which only highly confident, assertive, ambitious, and extroverted individuals would find success. Many in his department, including many women, embraced the characterization. And so, when hiring managers from marketing took part in *any* interviews—even for candidates not interviewing for their department—they tended to carry over their beliefs about what an "ideal" candidate looked like and to reject candidates on the basis of these arbitrary criteria.

Mystery solved. Does that mean it's time for unconscious bias training?

No, or at least, not yet. You won't be able to achieve DEI until you move beyond a simplistic view of "best practices" as your default answer to DEI challenges. Actually achieving DEI requires that you understand your organization inside and out, that you accurately conceptualize the arc of change-making with the level of trust you're working with, and that you solve the right problems.

Recall again the outcomes we're trying to achieve with DEI:

- Equity, the measured experience of individual, interpersonal, and organizational success and well-being across all stakeholder populations
- Diversity, the workforce demographic composition in an organizational body that all stakeholder populations trust as representative and accountable
- Inclusion, the felt and perceived environment in an organizational body that all stakeholder populations trust as respectful and accountable

There's a reason that trust is such a crucial component in these outcomes: the perception of an environment by the people in and around it is as important as any "objective" achievement of representational parity or engagement.

47. Lee, Stacy. "Promoting Diversity and Inclusion through Your Recruitment ATS." Business 2 Community, June 2, 2021. https://www.business2community.com/human -resources/promoting-diversity-and-inclusion-through -your-recruitment-ats-02409827.

33

Track Trust

Trust—the belief that when a leader makes a promise, it'll be kept—is the currency of any organizational change effort.[48] Trust buys patience, goodwill, understanding, and generosity, and organizations that are high in it are able to take on ambitious DEI initiatives that require the participation of the entire workforce and find success. But organizations lacking in trust face a unique set of challenges: less collaboration, vulnerability, and engagement and more apathy, hostility, and selfishness.

Given the extreme importance of trust, it's imperative to gauge whether an environment is high, medium, or low in trust. For example, it's impossible to use a survey to build a common case for change when no one trusts the organization enough to fill out the survey. Just as divers need to monitor their oxygen levels, practitioners working toward systems change need to monitor the amount of trust in the environment they're working within, and adjust their strategy accordingly.

PRACTITIONER'S TIP

Most organizations naively believe trust to be an infinite resource, when it most certainly is not. Every time employees are asked to share their experiences in a survey or public forum, that expends trust. Every time employees utilize a formal feedback mechanism or participate in a hiring process, they expend trust. If their stories are respected, suggestions respected, feedback taken, and best efforts recognized and evaluated fairly, the expended trust is renewed with interest, enabling organizations and practitioners to take even bigger actions. If trust is honored and respected, it enables a positive feedback loop of organizational functioning and change; if not, the well quickly runs dry. Keep this simple fact in mind as you seek to create systemic change as a practitioner, and use this exercise to assess the environments you seek to make change within.

LEARNING GOALS

- Learn how trust affects systemic change work and strategy.
- Measure trust and assess whether an environment is low, medium, or high trust.
- Apply trust-rebuilding strategies to your contexts.

UNDERSTAND YOURSELF

EXPAND YOUR CAPACITY

RELY ON OTHERS

FIND YOUR PLACE

DIAGNOSE INEQUITY

CHAMPION INCLUSION

ADDRESS CONFLICT AND HARM

ORGANIZE A MOVEMENT

REIMAGINE SYSTEMS

ACHIEVE DEI

INSTRUCTIONS

Learn about how the level of trust in an environment affects organizational change work. Then, follow the directions to assess the level of trust in different contexts, with different people and groups your DEI initiatives are working with, and modify your strategic approach across these contexts. Afterwards, answer the reflection questions.

Trust Is the Currency of Change

How can we tell whether an environment is high, medium, or low trust? An easy way is to measure people's reactions to leadership commitment. The greater the skepticism or cynicism, the lower the trust. Each type of environment has telltale symptoms, as well.

HIGH TRUST

In high-trust environments, when harm is committed, it is rectified swiftly and without incident. Feedback is shared casually and proactively regardless of seniority, title, or identity. People are patient when it comes to change and willing to extend the benefit of the doubt to each other amid challenges, and they assume that their interests are always in the mind of decision-makers. These outcomes result from a consistent leadership track record, effective responses to crises and controversies, and strong relationships between the people and groups in the organization.

MEDIUM TRUST

The biggest indicator of medium-trust environments is the clear presence of doubt—enough to call into question the ability of organizational leadership to actually achieve what they say they will, but not so much that people assume change will never happen. Stakeholders are skeptical but not yet *cynical* and will often challenge the official narrative put out by an organization, whether in public or private. These outcomes emerge from a less-than-spotless track record. While leaders may have tried to make amends for harm, their responses may not have been adequate. Some might have brushed off or dismissed incidents of mistreatment when reported, retaliated against whistle-blowers, or simply delayed taking action for far too long, and lost trust as a result.

LOW TRUST

Low-trust environments are not difficult to identify: they're defined almost entirely by cynicism. Numerous people and groups within the organization doubt organizational leadership, organizational processes, each other, and themselves. In these environments, trust is a sign of weakness, an opening to be exploited, and so behavior tends to degrade into apathy, hostility, sabotage, or self-interest. Low-trust organizations have become that way because repeated breaches of trust and repeated harm without accountability have convinced a critical mass that the organization is homogenous, inequitable, and exclusive because its leaders intend it to be so, and survival in such an environment is easier if one adopts the same toxicity as everyone else.

1. Choose one DEI-related issue or initiative to focus on throughout Exercises 33–36 that will require systemic change to address. It does not need to be one for which you have taken any steps on addressing or have gathered data. Name your issue or initiative below.

_____

_____

_____

2. On the following chart, name three contexts relevant to the DEI movement you're engaged in or planning. Then, answer the prompts to document evidence on whether the context is low, medium, or high trust, and indicate it in the final column.

CONTEXT What is the environment you're assessing?	EVIDENCE How do people react when things go wrong? How do people react to cynical statements about leaders or the environment? How do people react when leaders make ambitious commitments?	TRUST Given the evidence, what level of trust exists?
The US-based People Ops team of eight people	They're frustrated but not surprised when people complain about lack of promotion opportunities, since they see where the problems stem from but aren't being listened to. They're privately starting to get more cynical, and roll their eyes when leaders make commitments to do better, but still try to participate in new DEI initiatives in the hopes that things will change.	Medium, bordering on low trust

UNDERSTAND YOURSELF | EXPAND YOUR CAPACITY | RELY ON OTHERS | FIND YOUR PLACE | DIAGNOSE INEQUITY | CHAMPION INCLUSION | ADDRESS CONFLICT AND HARM | ORGANIZE A MOVEMENT | REIMAGINE SYSTEMS | ACHIEVE DEI

Trust-Rebuilding Strategies

When trust is medium or low, achieving systemic change often requires different strategies compared to a "normal" change-making effort, to mitigate unique challenges and rebuild that trust. Review the following strategies and the example in action.

MEDIUM-TRUST STRATEGIES		
STRATEGY	**DESCRIPTION**	**EFFECT**
Get skin in the game.	Back up commitments with consequences for failure.	Increases belief in accountability
Empower external accountability.	Create groups that have power to make choices and hold leaders accountable.	Increases efficacy by sharing power
Activate nonleader change-makers.	Encourage the formation of grassroots movements and bottom-up change.	Increases efficacy by sharing power
Make steady small wins.	Start with small goals and steadily scale efforts larger over time.	Builds a track record

LOW-TRUST STRATEGIES		
STRATEGY	**DESCRIPTION**	**EFFECT**
Let change find you.	Let those with the least power make the first move, and react to it with support.	Increases efficacy by ceding visibility
Apologize and cede power.	Give a genuine apology for past and present harm, and change behaviors.	Increases efficacy by sharing power
Movements lead the way.	Support grassroots movements with unconditional resources.	Builds goodwill
Use windows of opportunity.	Take swift, decisive, and at times radical action during moments of opportunity.	Builds goodwill and a track record

CONTEXT	TRUST	EXAMPLE TRUST-REBUILDING STRATEGY
US-based People Ops team of eight people	Medium, bordering on low trust	Leaders should apologize for past inaction and commit to a short-term audit with a third-party group whose analysis will be made public to the company. They can organize a working group open to the company with a large discretionary budget to collect additional feedback about promotion opportunities. Finally, they can set a public goal of bringing the average time between promotions to less than two years and give up bonuses if they fail.

3. Pick *one* of the contexts you named that is medium or low trust, and answer the prompts to create a unique trust-rebuilding strategy for that context.

CONTEXT What is the environment you're assessing?	TRUST What is the trust level of the context at present?	TRUST-REBUILDING STRATEGY How might you increase or rebuild trust in this context to increase the chances that your DEI effort will be successful, and why will these strategies be the most useful in your context?

REFLECTION QUESTIONS

1. After assessing environments relevant to your DEI effort, were you surprised by any of your conclusions regarding trust? Why or why not?

_____

_____

_____

2. How has this exercise changed how you're planning on working with different people and groups as part of your organizational change efforts, if at all? Why?

_____

_____

_____

UNDERSTAND YOURSELF

EXPAND YOUR CAPACITY

RELY ON OTHERS

FIND YOUR PLACE

DIAGNOSE INEQUITY

CHAMPION INCLUSION

ADDRESS CONFLICT AND HARM

ORGANIZE A MOVEMENT

REIMAGINE SYSTEMS

ACHIEVE DEI

3. It's always a possibility that the level of trust within an environment is so low that we aren't able to engage effectively with it. If this is or were to be the case with a group or context your movement was hoping to engage with, what would you do in that scenario?

_____

_____

_____

_____

4. Finally, it's often the case that as individuals we don't have the power needed to leverage or increase trust for a given environment. How might this exercise still be useful to us in that case?

_____

_____

_____

_____

NOTE

48. Sloyan, Robert M. Trust, _Sensemaking, and Individual Responses to Organizational Change._ Benedictine University, 2009.

" IF TRUST IS HONORED
AND RESPECTED,
IT ENABLES A POSITIVE
FEEDBACK LOOP OF
ORGANIZATIONAL
FUNCTIONING AND CHANGE;
IF NOT, THE WELL
QUICKLY RUNS DRY.

34

Craft a Theory of Change

If you've done your homework, you know how to quantify and describe where your organization is currently at: your "point A," and all the challenges and opportunities that define it. You also have an idea of your "point B," the more diverse, equitable, and inclusive future you're trying to create, and some key outcomes that define it. But bridging those two points is a different matter than identifying them and requires a more disciplined approach: one rooted in outcomes, with strong accountability, and embodying curiosity and humility as a practitioner.

The keystone of such an approach is a theory of change, a set of interconnected and concrete hypotheses that can help you identify and tailor initiatives that will achieve the impact you seek.[49] Why take the time to do this, even if it slows down our efforts? Because we want to ensure that we're not simply throwing the first initiative that comes to mind at a problem. A theory of change keeps us as practitioners accountable to the outcomes we want to create.

PRACTITIONER'S TIP

Wait! Before you proceed ahead, ask yourself if you are *truly* the first person in your organization or context to attempt to solve the big problem you've identified. Accurate theories of change are challenging to create because they require accurate and holistic understandings of complex problems. The long road of creating one requires building strong relationships with many different people affected by an issue and stress testing your assumptions. If there's any chance that anyone else completed all or some of these steps in the past, you can save yourself valuable time by learning from those who have come before you. This exercise will ask you many times to answer *how* and *why* certain outcomes result. The more you rely on others' past information gathering, the less work you need to do to reinvent the wheel.

LEARNING GOALS

- Create a cause-and-effect diagram for an issue your DEI effort is attempting to solve.
- Create a theory of change and the strategic initiatives related to it.

UNDERSTAND YOURSELF

EXPAND YOUR CAPACITY

RELY ON OTHERS

FIND YOUR PLACE

DIAGNOSE INEQUITY

CHAMPION INCLUSION

ADDRESS CONFLICT AND HARM

ORGANIZE A MOVEMENT

REIMAGINE SYSTEMS

ACHIEVE DEI

INSTRUCTIONS

Review the information on cause-and-effect diagrams. Then, fill out your own diagram for the issue your DEI effort is attempting to solve, and follow the directions to develop your unique theory of change. Afterwards, answer the reflection questions.

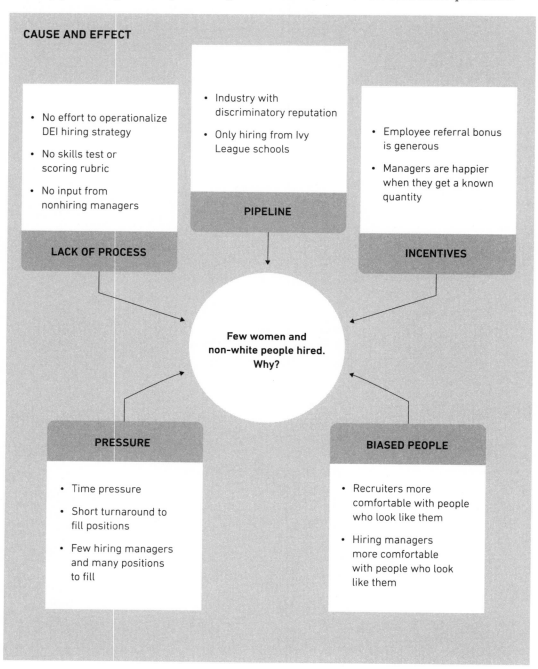

CAUSE AND EFFECT

LACK OF PROCESS
- No effort to operationalize DEI hiring strategy
- No skills test or scoring rubric
- No input from nonhiring managers

PIPELINE
- Industry with discriminatory reputation
- Only hiring from Ivy League schools

INCENTIVES
- Employee referral bonus is generous
- Managers are happier when they get a known quantity

Few women and non-white people hired. Why?

PRESSURE
- Time pressure
- Short turnaround to fill positions
- Few hiring managers and many positions to fill

BIASED PEOPLE
- Recruiters more comfortable with people who look like them
- Hiring managers more comfortable with people who look like them

Cause and Effect

A cause-and-effect diagram is one way to visualize possible causes behind a specific problem or outcome, grouping them by "theories" or families of smaller causes. Many kinds of cause-and-effect diagrams show the main effect or outcome being analyzed (shown here in the center circle); many different causes that contribute to the effect or outcome; and finally, column headers that group different "types" of causes. The following graphic shows an example of a cause-and-effect diagram for the outcome of "few women and non-White people hired" in an organization. Several contributing factors are named, and they are organized by five major themes or groups: pipeline, lack of process, biased people, pressure, and incentives.

Cause-and-effect diagrams are useful ways to help organize your thoughts into a theory of change: a set of interconnected and concrete hypotheses for changing one situation into another. Using this example, a detailed theory of change might be something like this:

> *We can increase the proportion of qualified new hires who are women and/or Black, Indigenous, Asian, Latine, or mixed by expanding the schools we hire from, designing a more rigorous hiring process, aligning our incentives around employee referral, easing time pressure on hiring managers, and training recruiters, hiring managers, and managers to understand how our DEI hiring efforts strengthen the organization.*

1. In this exercise, you'll create your own cause-and-effect diagram for your DEI effort and use it to create your unique theory of change. First, begin by naming the negative outcome that your effort intends to address or change below.

_____

_____

2. Then, brainstorm causes or contributing factors to this negative outcome. Why is this issue persisting? How did it come about? What needs to be changed for this outcome to change?

_____

_____

_____

_____

3. Organize these contributing factors into up to four major groups—types of causes. Name each major group, and make it a column heading in the following chart. Then list each group's contributing factors below it. A sample is provided.

LITTLE PROCESS				
▪ No input from nonhiring managers ▪ No skills test or scoring rubric ▪ No effort to use hiring strategy				

Now, invert your contributing factors to brainstorm initiatives for a theory of change. For example, if a contributing factor to inequity is "no input from nonhiring managers," you might invert it to "integrate input from nonhiring managers into the process."

BETTER PROCESS				
▪ Integrate input from nonhiring managers ▪ Develop a skills test and rubric ▪ Intentionally use a hiring strategy				

Use your answers to complete the empty diagram. Write the outcome or effect your issue is addressing in the center circle, put the group names for the contributing factors and causes in the column headers, and fill in each branch of the diagram with the individual contributing factors you identified. Then write the theory of change that you outlined initiatives for in the empty box.

THEORY OF CHANGE

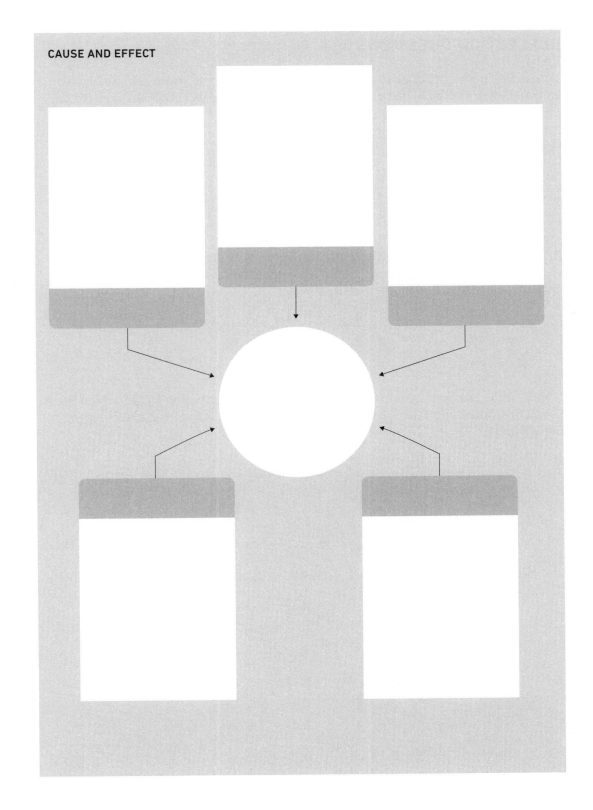

CAUSE AND EFFECT

REFLECTION QUESTIONS

1. How will the Theory of Change and cause-and-effect diagram you created help with your DEI efforts? Which, if any, of your plans or next steps will you modify based on these exercises?

_____

_____

_____

_____

2. The more parties that weigh in on a cause-and-effect diagram, the more accurate it and the theory of change you develop from it will be. How might you best seek out additional feedback and input, and from whom?

_____

_____

_____

3. Review the initiatives you created by inverting the contributing factors to the issue. For each group of initiatives you created, which do you think will have the biggest impact and why?

_____

_____

_____

_____

4. If you were to use the information in this exercise to equip a DEI-related movement, how might you best do that?

_____

_____

_____

_____

5. How has this exercise changed how you're planning on working with different people and groups as part of your organizational change efforts, if at all? What additional parties have you identified through this exercise that you might engage with?

NOTE

49. United Nations Development Group. "Theory of Change UNDAF Companion Guidance." United Nations Development Group, June 2017. https://unsdg.un.org/sites/default/files/UNDG-UNDAF-Companion-Pieces-7-Theory-of-Change.pdf.

UNDERSTAND YOURSELF

EXPAND YOUR CAPACITY

RELY ON OTHERS

FIND YOUR PLACE

DIAGNOSE INEQUITY

CHAMPION INCLUSION

ADDRESS CONFLICT AND HARM

ORGANIZE A MOVEMENT

REIMAGINE SYSTEMS

ACHIEVE DEI

35

Create a DEI Strategy

A theory of change helps us understand how we might address the various factors underlying a negative outcome to shift it toward a positive one. But this isn't the same thing as a *strategy*: a concrete plan, with a set of clear initiatives, efforts, and timelines, for achieving a desired *set of outcomes*, accompanied by guidance on the trade-offs and reprioritization of other outcomes that are acceptable in the pursuit of these. A strategy tells us what matters, how it matters in relation to everything else, and how we'll achieve it.[50] Within DEI work, it's a DEI strategy that allows us to hold leaders accountable and measure our progress.

The best DEI strategies divert heavily from cookie cutter strategies you might find online ("focus on hiring a diverse workforce and invest in retention!"). The best strategies are heavily tailored for a given organization or context and make use of all the information you've gathered about your context: the level of trust available to you, the coalitions possible to create, and everything you know from diagnosing inequities. These things all come together in a DEI strategy.

PRACTITIONER'S TIP

Effective strategies are less about comprehensiveness and more about prioritization. It might be possible, for example, to come up with a list of 100 DEI initiatives that might together turn any organization around—but no organization will have the time, money, or political will to do anything close to that. Embedded in a good strategy is a set of critical assumptions about what kinds of efforts maximize feasibility, impact, and visibility at a given point in time to best ensure success, and these assumptions should shift and change as the organization and the moment do as well.

LEARNING GOALS

- Identify the key elements of a DEI strategy for your own DEI effort: key outcomes, relevant parties, DEI initiatives, and DEI tactics.
- Gain experience creating a comprehensive DEI strategy.

UNDERSTAND YOURSELF

EXPAND YOUR CAPACITY

RELY ON OTHERS

FIND YOUR PLACE

DIAGNOSE INEQUITY

CHAMPION INCLUSION

ADDRESS CONFLICT AND HARM

ORGANIZE A MOVEMENT

REIMAGINE SYSTEMS

ACHIEVE DEI

INSTRUCTIONS

Follow the exercise questions to identify the key outcomes you want to achieve and the corresponding relevant parties and theory of change. Answer the questions to brainstorm unique DEI initiatives and modify them with trust and tactics in mind. Finally, put these pieces together to complete your unique DEI strategy. Each question in this exercise will have a sample answer *in italics* immediately following it.

1. This exercise starts simple. Name the broader organization, community, or environment that you will focus on for this exercise and design a DEI strategy for.

> **A.** *Typical Corporation Inc.*

2. Name the *most important* interconnected issues or inequities in this environment that inspired this DEI effort. These should be high-level issues that manifest as numerous DEI symptoms.

> **B.** *An enduring lack of gender and racial representation at all levels and the rapid turnover of women and non-White people.*

3. Review the many kinds of DEI outcomes, and pick *three key outcomes* that you aim to achieve to address the issues or inequities you listed.

DEI Outcomes

Representational Parity A demographic composition at every level of seniority, within every department, and for every role that mirrors constituent demographics	**Representational Support** The collective sense of feeling represented and supported by leaders, regardless of leaders' overall demographic composition	**Multicultural Environment** An environment with a high level of variety in people's identities, cultures, and backgrounds
Kindred Environment An environment with a high level of similarity in people's identities, cultures, and backgrounds	**Mixed Environment** An environment with pockets of high variety or similarity in people's identities, cultures, and backgrounds	**Accessible Environment** The collective sense of being able to participate fully in the workplace and in workplace processes as a result of having access needs met

Accountable Resolution Conflict resolution processes that are resolved fairly and satisfactorily, ensure accountability, and protect dignity for all parties	**Agency** The collective comfort and confidence to show up however authentically or not in an environment	**Authenticity** The collective expression of people's "authentic self" in an environment
Belonging The collective sense of feeling part of a greater whole and "part of the group" within an environment	**Community** The collective sense of having access to groups of people willing to provide mutual support and companionship	**Decision-Making** The collective sense of inclusion within decision-making processes and that shared feedback is valued and utilized
Enablement The collective sense of being equipped and resourced to successfully and sustainably fulfill responsibilities	**Engagement** High participation and buy-in for workplace processes and initiatives, and a sense of fulfillment from work	**Equitable Evaluation** An evaluation process that does not intentionally or unintentionally benefit some types of workers over others
Equitable Hiring A hiring process that does not intentionally or unintentionally benefit some types of candidates over others	**Equitable Promoting** A promotion process that does not intentionally or unintentionally benefit some types of candidates over others	**Ethical Behavior** Practices and relationships with institutions and workers that avoid nepotism, corruption, theft, and abuse
Fair Labor The collective sense of being rewarded fairly for the effort and quality of work delivered and being treated without abuse or exploitation	**Inclusion** The collective sense of feeling respected and valued within an environment	**Non-exceptionalism** The ability for all workers to fulfill their responsibilities and be "average" without fear of repercussions
Privacy and Security The ability to control how information is collected and used, and the protections safeguarding this information	**Professional Growth** Tailored learning and development, challenging opportunities, and fair career progression for everyone	**Psychological Safety** An environment where people feel free to take risks, share critical feedback, and fail without fear of retaliation
Purpose The collective sense of contributing to an important purpose and mission through work	**Social Justice** Leveraging of an organization's brand, platform, and resources to participate in social movements and achieve social justice	**Sustainability** The ability to operate without depleting natural resources needed to ensure a stable future
Transparency The collective understanding of an organization's operations, successes, and failures as a result of information sharing	**Trust** The collective sense of trusting the organization's leadership and processes to achieve what they purport to	**Universal Design** The collective sense of feeling included and able to utilize a product or service as intended
Well-Being An environment that sustains and supports the physical needs and mental health of everyone in it	**Work Flexibility** The collective sense of being able to work however, whenever, and wherever people want so long as work outcomes are achieved	**Work–Life Balance** The collective sense of feeling able to set boundaries between work and nonwork, and have those boundaries respected

C. *Representational parity, inclusion, accountable resolution*

4. What broad strategic focuses would allow you to achieve the three outcomes you chose? If you were to name distinct categories to spend money, time, and effort on, what would these be?

D. *Hiring and recruitment, respectful workplace norms, reporting and accountability*

5. Name no more than *five initiatives* on a more granular level within your broad strategic focuses that would allow you to achieve the outcomes you named.

E. *(1) Piloting mutually beneficial programs at women's colleges; historically Black colleges and universities; and Asian, Black, Native American, and Latine professional organizations. (2) Mitigating bias in our hiring processes. (3) Creating shared organization-wide expectations for respectful communication. (4) Training managers to reinforce values with their teams and model conflict resolution. (5) Expanding our informal reporting process using a third-party reporting platform.*

6. Which constituents or parties would these initiatives depend on for funding, leadership, or participation?

> **F.** *The entire People Ops and learning & development departments, all managers, senior leadership, and the board of directors*

7. What considerations should these initiatives keep in mind, given the power and agenda of these parties and the level of trust you're working with?

> **G.** *Due to distrust of DEI efforts from past failures, we should take a "small wins" approach to show success. Prioritize the initiative to set organization-wide expectations, but start by running a campaign to highlight and celebrate the managers with the most respectful and inclusive teams to build interest. If this succeeds, we can leverage this into management training that excites leaders and sets up the other initiatives for future years.*

UNDERSTAND YOURSELF

EXPAND YOUR CAPACITY

RELY ON OTHERS

FIND YOUR PLACE

DIAGNOSE INEQUITY

CHAMPION INCLUSION

ADDRESS CONFLICT AND HARM

ORGANIZE A MOVEMENT

REIMAGINE SYSTEMS

ACHIEVE DEI

8. Finally, combine your answers A–G into a single, coherent DEI strategy.

> *Typical Corporation Inc. (A) struggles with an enduring lack of gender and racial representation at all levels and the rapid turnover of women and non-White people (B). We must achieve representational parity, inclusion, and accountable conflict resolution (C) and will do so by building more respectful workplace norms, strengthening reporting and accountability, and reimagining our approach to hiring and recruitment (D). We will start by creating shared organization-wide expectations for respectful communication and by training managers to reinforce values with their teams and model conflict resolution (E). These efforts will involve the People Ops and learning & development departments, all managers, and senior leadership most heavily (F), but they won't succeed unless we all get involved. We'll start with these initiatives, but there will be much more to come (G).*

NOTE

50. Watkins, Michael D. "Demystifying Strategy: The What, Who, How, and Why." Harvard Business Review, September 10, 2007. https://hbr.org/2007/09/demystifying-strategy-the-what.

" A STRATEGY TELLS US WHAT MATTERS, HOW IT MATTERS IN RELATION TO EVERYTHING ELSE, AND HOW WE'LL ACHIEVE IT.

36

Measure, Measure, Measure

Measuring success starts with measuring anything at all, and that takes us to the importance of data and metrics. Many DEI metrics exist, measuring infrastructure, career growth and progression, interpersonal interaction, misconduct, well-being, representation, social and environmental impact, belonging, and so much more. But metrics are challenging to identify, measure, and analyze; few organizations can afford to measure *everything*.

Rather than checking boxes on a laundry list of metrics out of context, skilled practitioners home in on the metrics that correspond with their initiatives—organized by a theory of change—and refine them into direct and proxy metrics that can accurately capture the outcomes they seek.

PRACTITIONER'S TIP

No matter how you feel about an initiative, you can't know for certain that it's "working" until you're able to measure that it's working. This is counterintuitive, especially because we're inclined to see isolated moments (grateful comments, inspirational stories) as indicators of more systemic success. It takes discipline and humility to take in these positive data points *and* maintain our focus on the metrics most able to capture our success or not, and to take action on that data as needed. It's surprisingly easy for an initiative that's well received to quietly fail at creating the change it was designed for, and for an initiative that gets little attention to result in a stunning success behind the scenes. Use this exercise to back up any initiative you design with metrics that help you hold yourself and leaders accountable for success and give you valuable data on effectiveness.

LEARNING GOALS

- Identify direct and proxy metrics related to an outcome.
- Create a plan to capture these metrics.

INSTRUCTIONS

Learn about metrics and the difference between direct and proxy metrics from the following text. Answer the exercise questions to identify direct and proxy metrics related to an initiative and a theory of change, and create a plan for regularly measuring progress.

Direct and Proxy Metrics

A **metric** is anything you measure to gain a better understanding of something. We can think of metrics as taking two forms: a **direct metric** gives you information on the precise outcome you're interested in, while a **proxy metric** gives you information on outcomes that are related to, but not exactly, the outcome you seek.[51] While direct metrics are the most accurate, they can often be difficult, costly, or otherwise challenging to measure. Proxy metrics run the risk of being less accurate, but if you select the right ones, they can be dramatically more convenient, low-cost, and otherwise easy to measure.

For example, if I wanted to measure the inclusiveness of the language in my job listings for job seekers, my *direct metric* would be "perceptions of language inclusiveness from job seekers," and I'd simply ask job seekers this question during the application process. But I may not get many responses, and asking this question itself might be difficult or awkward to implement. I might recognize this and set a *proxy metric* of "rates of application from job seekers with a range of identities," inferring that if the language were seen as more inclusive, a greater range of people would apply to the position. This proxy metric might not be perfect, but it'd be easier to measure simply by looking at the aggregate demographics of the candidates who apply to a role.

How does one select the "right" proxy metrics? By developing an accurate *theory of change* in partnership with a varied set of people and groups. Because a theory of change is a series of interconnected hypotheses developed from your knowledge about the organization and the issue you're tackling, the more accurate these hypotheses, the more accurate the proxy metrics you reverse-engineer from them.

For example, if I'm trying to create an outcome of increased employee trust in the organization and have created a theory of change that links increased trust to rewarding employee vulnerability, taking action in response to employee feedback, and involving employees in decision-making, then my proxy metrics might focus on measuring employee vulnerability, feedback, and engagement. More specifically, I might pick "the number of constructively critical comments shared in all-company meetings," "the amount of employee feedback volunteered during open comment periods for proposed new policies, processes, or initiatives," and "overall employee engagement, measured in a monthly pulse survey" on top of my direct metric of "employee perceptions of trust." We may not always be able to pick our own direct metric, but we often *do* have the ability to choose proxy metrics. Knowing how to use both helps us make the most of the data we gather.

1. Fill in the following chart with a DEI outcome, your theory of change to achieve it, and the direct and proxy metrics you might select to gauge progress on it. A sample answer begins the chart.

OUTCOME	THEORY OF CHANGE	DIRECT METRICS	PROXY METRICS
Increased employee trust	We can increase employee trust by rewarding vulnerability, taking action utilizing employee feedback, and involving employees in decisions.	Employee perceptions of trust	Number of critical comments in all company meetings; feedback volunteered in open comment periods; monthly employee engagement

2. How might you collect data on your direct metric(s)? What might be the most realistic or feasible way to collect this data, if there are several, and how often will you collect it?

_____

_____

_____

3. How might you collect data on your proxy metrics? If you have multiple proxy metrics, what forms will they take, and how often will you collect data?

_____

_____

_____

4. How might your direct and proxy metrics be used together to demonstrate success or not? What are you looking for, more specifically?

_____

_____

_____

_____

UNDERSTAND YOURSELF

EXPAND YOUR CAPACITY

RELY ON OTHERS

FIND YOUR PLACE

DIAGNOSE INEQUITY

CHAMPION INCLUSION

ADDRESS CONFLICT AND HARM

ORGANIZE A MOVEMENT

REIMAGINE SYSTEMS

ACHIEVE DEI

5. Who in your organization will collect and utilize this data? If not you directly, how will you hold leaders and anyone else who might use this data accountable?

_____

_____

_____

_____

NOTE

51. Sweeney, Rose. "What the Heck Is a Proxy Metric and Why You Care." FactorLab, October 23, 2020. https://factorlab.com/what-the-heck-is-a-proxy-metric-and-why-you-care.

" IT'S SURPRISINGLY EASY
FOR AN INITIATIVE THAT'S
WELL RECEIVED TO QUIETLY
FAIL AT CREATING THE CHANGE
IT WAS DESIGNED FOR, AND
FOR AN INITIATIVE THAT GETS
LITTLE ATTENTION TO RESULT
IN A STUNNING SUCCESS
BEHIND THE SCENES.

ACHIEVE DEI

As many practitioners say, DEI work never truly "ends." It's a saying that's intended to help us to stay on our toes, to not grow complacent, and to not assume that just because we've organized a few successful events and initiatives, the work is done. But sometimes this sentiment can feel exhausting,

> ❝ IT TAKES EFFORT TO STEADILY LEARN FROM THE PAST AND DOCUMENT THE PRESENT, SO THAT WE MIGHT CONTINUALLY CREATE BETTER FUTURES

especially to those who feel like actually achieving diversity, equity, and inclusion is so far away as to be functionally impossible. To those, I want to say unequivocally:

> *It is possible to achieve diversity, equity, and inclusion as outcomes. And yes, there is an end goal for this work: an organization, community, or environment where every person feels seen and represented, experiences the presence of success and well-being and the absence of discrimination, and feels respected and valued for who they are.*

If we lose track of this goal as a real possibility, disillusionment isn't far behind. If we lose faith in our ability to improve, our efforts will build bridges to nowhere until the people building them burn out, and when we do succeed, we won't even know. If we lose our memory of what we've achieved and how, the momentum of change will disappear, alongside our perspective of what's possible. If we lose faith in our movements existing over the long term, they'll fizzle out, leaving those who come after us to retrace our steps again and again without achieving change. And worst of all, if we forget to keep track of ourselves, *we'll* be the ones who fizzle out, and all our skills will be for nothing.

Achieving DEI is possible. And we should believe in its possibility so sincerely that we take seriously the need to *sustain* it over time, because in that sense, the work doesn't end. It takes effort to be able to recognize when things aren't good enough, to intervene in order to fix them, and to gauge improvement so that we know our intervention was successful. It takes effort to steadily learn from the past and document the present, so that we might continually create better futures. It takes effort to not only build movements, but sustain their momentum over time so that they can continue achieving change even if their members cycle out. And it takes effort to be able to proudly reflect on how far we've come, while still recognizing how far we need to go—not just aspirationally, but operationally.

Finally, we need to recognize that no matter how much we care about this work, it's still work. Like all workers, DEI practitioners and inclusive leaders run the risk of burnout—even more so if we're passionate about what we do, and less strict about our own boundaries. Being in this work for the long haul requires that we train ourselves for how to do that and that we make time for experiences that we might only experience rarely if we left it up to chance: rest and joy.

37

Gauge Maturity

DEI work might be nonlinear, but we can think of organizations' DEI progress through the lens of a maturity model: a tool that allows us to track an organization's growth and development, from centering DEI intentions to achieving DEI outcomes on foundational, internal, and external levels. Most organizations start off with actions and initiatives that are easy to create and utilize, but these actions themselves aren't enough to create changed outcomes. Over time, however, as organizations grow in their DEI capabilities, they become increasingly able to use data, align people-related systems, activate leaders, and create external impact that matches their values.

The simple maturity model described in this exercise is a way to start assessing the extent to which your organization's foundational, internal, and external DEI practices are where they need to be to achieve the outcomes you seek.

PRACTITIONER'S TIP

Models like the one introduced in this section are rarely perfectly applicable to every organization, but they can offer new ways to think about the work you're already doing. This maturity model focuses most on trust and value. The further up in the maturity model one goes, the more valuable the actions, but the more expensive the cost, referring to the trust required to execute them. The more trust an organization is able to build, the more trust an organization is able to leverage, and the better an organization will be able to achieve its foundational, internal, and external DEI outcomes. Use this exercise to periodically check your progress and hold yourself and your organization accountable for change.

LEARNING GOALS

- Understand how trust, organizational value, and DEI maturity relate to each other in a four-step DEI maturity model.
- Assess your own organization's progress toward DEI on foundational, internal, and external dimensions.

INSTRUCTIONS

Read The Four Levels of Achieving DEI, then answer the exercise questions to assess where your organization lies on its DEI foundation, internal aspects, and external aspects. Afterwards, answer the reflection questions.

The Four Levels of Achieving DEI

Organizations that have been able to achieve diversity, equity, and inclusion as out-comes use dramatically different tools to do so than do organizations that are still at the beginning stages. The biggest difference in these tools is the trust they require to execute: the most impactful DEI efforts for both constituents and the organization as a whole are those that require universal buy-in, vulnerability, and participation—things that you only get when there's trust to spare.

LEVEL 1

Level 1 of DEI maturity is characterized by actions that have no prerequisites to their execution or implementation. These are actions that might range in scope and scale, but the common factor across them is that they are often taken reactively or are being done for their own sake. They require little in the way of formal commitment or buy-in to implement, whether from leaders or from employees or workers, and so it's difficult for these efforts to "fail." However, level 1 actions done well can build the trust needed to reach level 2. Examples include creating DEI mission statements, celebrating cultural holidays, and offering opt-in DEI resources.

LEVEL 2

Level 2 of DEI maturity is characterized by an increasing amount of *interdependence*: actions that fall into level 2 typically require that constituents buy in and have a role in deciding the outcomes. Because they involve many more people, there is a chance of failure if those involved decide that the efforts aren't effective enough, but overall these efforts still constitute relatively basic first steps at collective DEI work. Level 2 actions done well can build the trust needed to reach level 3, and examples include hiring DEI professionals, organizing employee resource groups and affinity groups, and voluntarily working with third-party benchmarking organizations and auditors.

LEVEL 3

Level 3 of DEI maturity is where outcomes start to come into the picture. Programs are created that take a higher degree of buy-in from multiple parties, with larger consequences for failure. External actions are undertaken in alignment with internal values, and with oversight. DEI data begins to be used for high-level strategy and in the services or products an organization offers, and some of this data is shared externally to constituents outside the organization as well. Organizations at level 3 are able to create DEI outcomes on many levels. If they continue building and leveraging trust, however, they're able to go even further.

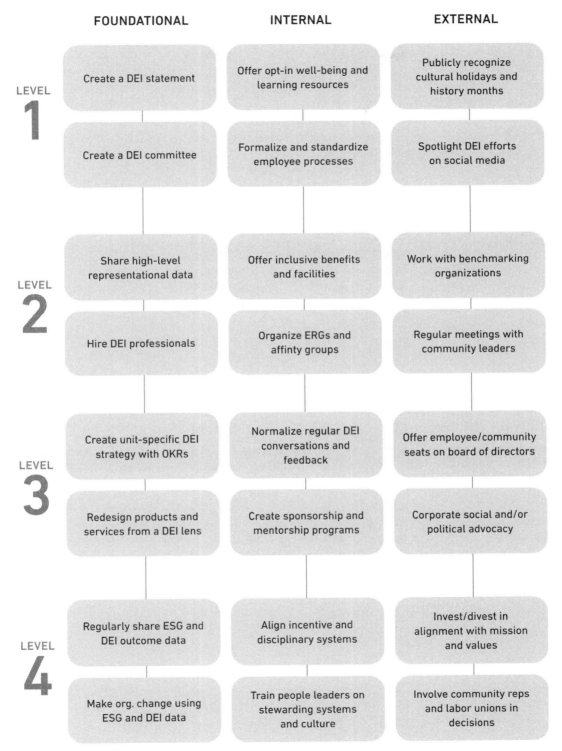

	FOUNDATIONAL	INTERNAL	EXTERNAL
LEVEL 1	Create a DEI statement	Offer opt-in well-being and learning resources	Publicly recognize cultural holidays and history months
	Create a DEI committee	Formalize and standardize employee processes	Spotlight DEI efforts on social media
LEVEL 2	Share high-level representational data	Offer inclusive benefits and facilities	Work with benchmarking organizations
	Hire DEI professionals	Organize ERGs and affinty groups	Regular meetings with community leaders
LEVEL 3	Create unit-specific DEI strategy with OKRs	Normalize regular DEI conversations and feedback	Offer employee/community seats on board of directors
	Redesign products and services from a DEI lens	Create sponsorship and mentorship programs	Corporate social and/or political advocacy
LEVEL 4	Regularly share ESG and DEI outcome data	Align incentive and disciplinary systems	Invest/divest in alignment with mission and values
	Make org. change using ESG and DEI data	Train people leaders on stewarding systems and culture	Involve community reps and labor unions in decisions

UNDERSTAND YOURSELF

EXPAND YOUR CAPACITY

RELY ON OTHERS

FIND YOUR PLACE

DIAGNOSE INEQUITY

CHAMPION INCLUSION

ADDRESS CONFLICT AND HARM

ORGANIZE A MOVEMENT

REIMAGINE SYSTEMS

ACHIEVE DEI

LEVEL 4

Level 4 of DEI maturity represents the most effective and high-value initiatives any organization can do with regard to DEI. They include regular collection, usage, and sharing of comprehensive DEI and ESG (environmental, social, and governance) data, the full activation of leaders within the organization to achieve strategy goals, and the strong participation of extra-organizational constituents to weigh in on activities. These activities are only possible with a workforce that fully believes in these actions, can clearly see the impact they create, and sees the effort needed for their success as normal and universally beneficial.

1. Reflect on your organization's foundational DEI practices—the structure and strategy by which it aims to achieve DEI work—and indicate the number of the statement that best describes your organization. _____

1	2	3	4
My organization has only stated an intention to do DEI work but has yet to develop a formal program, strategy, or goals.	My organization is beginning to bring in professionals and has some idea about what it wants to address, but no clear goals yet.	My organization has clear goals for what it wants to address, has created a clear strategy to do so, and supports people with the job to execute it.	My organization can track granular progress toward its goals, uses DEI data in all its decisions, and regularly updates its DEI strategy.

2. Reflect on your organization's internal DEI practices—the way DEI work manifests inside of your organization—and indicate the number of the statement that best describes your organization. _____

1	2	3	4
My organization relies primarily on volunteers to create whatever DEI-related programming or initiatives occur.	My organization is beginning to leverage its resources to support employee needs and encourage employee-organized groups.	My organization is investing in many programs and initiatives to create an inclusive, equitable, and diverse working environment.	My organization has successfully built a self-sustaining environment where diversity, equity, and inclusion are built and maintained by all.

3. Reflect on your organization's external DEI practices—the way DEI work manifests outside of your organization—and indicate the number of the statement that best describes your organization. _____

1	2	3	4
My organization uses DEI primarily as marketing and branding to engage those outside the organization.	My organization is beginning to engage in transparency efforts and starting conversations with constituents outside of the organization.	My organization is using its resources to advocate externally on important issues and sharing info and some power with constituents.	My organization acts as if its survival and that of its constituents are one and the same, and it leverages its resources and power with this in mind.

4. Add up the numbers you indicated, and divide the final answer by three to identify your organization's DEI maturity from one to four. _____

REFLECTION QUESTIONS

1. Did your organization's overall DEI maturity, or the maturity of its foundational, internal, and external DEI aspects, surprise you? Why or why not?

_____

_____

_____

2. What DEI initiatives and efforts has your organization undertaken recently, and how have those efforts changed your organization's rating on any of these aspects?

_____

_____

_____

3. What would need to change most for your organization to move up to the next level of maturity? Be as specific as possible in your answer.

_____

_____

_____

UNDERSTAND YOURSELF

EXPAND YOUR CAPACITY

RELY ON OTHERS

FIND YOUR PLACE

DIAGNOSE INEQUITY

CHAMPION INCLUSION

ADDRESS CONFLICT AND HARM

ORGANIZE A MOVEMENT

REIMAGINE SYSTEMS

ACHIEVE DEI

4. Think of a few colleagues in your organization. Would they agree with your assessment? If they would disagree, why, and where would the biggest disagreement be?

_____

_____

_____

_____

5. Which of these aspects—foundational, internal, or external—is your organization strongest at vs. weakest at? How might it build on its strengths to mitigate its weaknesses?

_____

_____

_____

_____

" THE MORE TRUST
AN ORGANIZATION IS ABLE
TO BUILD, THE MORE TRUST
AN ORGANIZATION IS ABLE
TO LEVERAGE, AND THE
BETTER AN ORGANIZATION WILL
BE ABLE TO ACHIEVE
ITS FOUNDATIONAL,
INTERNAL, AND EXTERNAL
DEI OUTCOMES.

38

Document Your Knowledge

The difference between the you reading this exercise and the you who first picked up this workbook is, most of all, knowledge. Throughout this workbook, you went through an accelerated version of the process all DEI practitioners experience: finding yourself, building skills, learning more about your organization, and putting it all together to start driving change. But even if you've built a strong movement and are surrounded by colleagues committed to achieving the same mission, can you confidently say that if you disappeared tomorrow, people would have everything they needed to carry on the work without you?

If the answer to that question is anything other than "absolutely yes," then you'll probably benefit from better documentation and knowledge transfer. It sounds routine, I know! Nobody wants to do paperwork when there's organizational change to enact. But without knowledge transfer or documentation, the departure of even one person from a DEI effort, if they are the only person who possesses institutional knowledge, can single-handedly end that effort. No one wants that.

PRACTITIONER'S TIP

There are two ingredients to successfully maintaining institutional memory: good recording and documentation, *and* strong norms, routines, and habits that teach and pass down this information to newcomers.[52] If we are the ones documenting information for the first time in our organization, or even just for ourselves, we need to be thinking ahead to how we want this information to be absorbed and learned in the future. Use standard and accessible formats and formatting, write in language that speaks to your future reader, and structure your thoughts (no word salad!). Use this exercise as a set of prompts to periodically reflect on and document your own institutional knowledge.

LEARNING GOALS

- Document the institutional knowledge related to your ongoing DEI efforts.
- Refresh your knowledge preservation practices related to your DEI work.

UNDERSTAND YOURSELF

EXPAND YOUR CAPACITY

RELY ON OTHERS

FIND YOUR PLACE

DIAGNOSE INEQUITY

CHAMPION INCLUSION

ADDRESS CONFLICT AND HARM

ORGANIZE A MOVEMENT

REIMAGINE SYSTEMS

ACHIEVE DEI

INSTRUCTIONS

Read Institutional Knowledge, then answer the exercise questions to document knowledge related to your DEI efforts and make plans to utilize this knowledge.

Institutional Knowledge

Institutional knowledge refers to the often unspoken knowledge about an organization's history, change over time, memory, insights, skills, tactics, and relationships that the longest-serving members of organizations often possess and that long-standing groups or entities within an organization aim to document and preserve. This is no different for DEI work. The knowledge that one of your organization's senior leaders likes to eat lunch at a certain restaurant on a certain day? Unbelievably valuable information for an advocate with an important message to share. The knowledge that your organization's "anonymous hotline" goes to an HR team that has historically ignored this information? Unbelievably valuable information for a new employee getting a lay of the land.

To capture institutional knowledge, you'll need to encourage knowledge sharing and documentation. If you've been filling out this workbook, this workbook itself will live as a source of institutional knowledge documenting your own journey! This exercise asks several questions to take this practice even further. Whether we document our answers in written form, video, or another format, these answers are necessary to ensure that those who come after us don't spend time or energy reinventing the wheel and trying to regain our hard-earned knowledge from scratch.

1. What are we trying to address, and why are we trying to address it?

_____

_____

_____

_____

2. What have we achieved, and how did we achieve it?

_____

_____

_____

_____

3. What have we learned, and how did we learn it?

_____

_____

_____

_____

4. What did we struggle with, and why did we struggle with it?

_____

_____

_____

_____

5. Whose efforts did we build on, and how did we build on them?

_____

_____

_____

_____

6. What was our strategy, and why was it effective (or not)?

_____

_____

_____

_____

7. Who did we work with, and how did we work with them?

_____

_____

_____

_____

UNDERSTAND YOURSELF

EXPAND YOUR CAPACITY

RELY ON OTHERS

FIND YOUR PLACE

DIAGNOSE INEQUITY

CHAMPION INCLUSION

ADDRESS CONFLICT AND HARM

ORGANIZE A MOVEMENT

REIMAGINE SYSTEMS

ACHIEVE DEI

8. What remains to be done, and how might we achieve it?

_____

_____

_____

_____

9. Finally, reflect on the information you just documented. How do you intend to document and utilize it so that people who want to learn about it can and will far into the future?

_____

_____

_____

_____

_____

_____

_____

_____

NOTE

52. MasterClass. "Institutional Knowledge: How to Transfer Institutional Memory." MasterClass, January 6, 2022. https://www.masterclass.com/articles/institutional-knowledge-guide.

" CAN YOU CONFIDENTLY SAY THAT IF YOU DISAPPEARED TOMORROW, PEOPLE WOULD HAVE EVERYTHING THEY NEEDED TO CARRY ON THE WORK WITHOUT YOU?

39

Future-Proof Movements

Systems change takes time and energy, no matter how effective we are at our work or how smartly we design our movements. The vast majority of organizations have existed for far longer than we have made efforts to bend them toward greater diversity, equity, and inclusion. Practitioners almost always have to grapple with the reality that our efforts to create the change we want to see might take not days, weeks, or months, but months, years, and possibly even decades.

If we are working alone, perhaps even seeing ourselves as the sole hero that will fix our organizations, this realization can be crushing. But for those of us who are committed to working together to achieve outcomes over all else, the time scale of systems change is just another design challenge to respond to. If progress takes time and energy, then we simply have to organize our efforts to sustain progress for as long a time and as much an effort as it takes.

> **PRACTITIONER'S TIP**
>
> It's a common habit to leave self-care, which ideally would be an ongoing and regular habit, until things have gotten so bad that it becomes a necessity. A similar statement could be said about succession planning: we neglect to look for our replacements or successors until we're forced to do so, and then we spend significant amounts of time stressing out about how we might condense months or years of mentorship and support into days and weeks. If you're in a leadership position, even an informal one, recognize that it's never too early to start thinking about the future of your movement and creating a succession plan. And the broader and more interdependent your movement, the more people you'll know who might be prime candidates to carry on the leadership mantle. Use this exercise as part of your succession planning process so that when the moment comes to transition leaders, it comes as a surprise to no one.

LEARNING GOALS

- Learn about effective succession planning.
- Create a succession plan, and identify succession candidates.
- Plan out a conversation with a succession candidate.

UNDERSTAND YOURSELF

EXPAND YOUR CAPACITY

RELY ON OTHERS

FIND YOUR PLACE

DIAGNOSE INEQUITY

CHAMPION INCLUSION

ADDRESS CONFLICT AND HARM

ORGANIZE A MOVEMENT

REIMAGINE SYSTEMS

ACHIEVE DEI

INSTRUCTIONS

Learn about succession planning, then answer the exercise questions to create your own succession plan, identify succession candidates, and reach out to them. Afterwards, answer the reflection questions.

Succession Planning

No matter who you are or what you're working on, chances are low that you'll be working on the same thing, in the same capacity, for the same organization in 10 years. If our movements and change-making efforts aren't resilient and long-lasting enough to survive without us, then they will always run the risks of living and dying through our participation. Good succession planning—essentially, working to make ourselves obsolete by passing down our expertise and wisdom to others who will take on a leadership role—allows our movements to outlive our participation in them.[53]

To engage in succession planning, we need to be constantly building strong relationships with other people who share our vision and are equally as committed to carrying it out. The ideal successors are thoughtful enough to learn from our institutional knowledge, but not so rigid that they're unable to do things differently from how we have. Then, after we've identified people whose long-term goals align with ours, we need to start working with them to make that transition seamless. That looks like actively training and mentoring them to gain the skills that they'll need, and steadily increasing their participation and responsibilities while slowly phasing out our own. Eventually, we'll make the formal flip and step down as leaders—and it will be largely symbolic, because at that point the successor will already, for all intents and purposes, have become a new leader.

1. Thinking about the DEI work you are undertaking or have undertaken in your organization, what would happen if you were to leave? What does that tell you about the work that depends on you?

---

2. What are the key skills that you use to succeed in this work? How did you gain them?

---

3. What is your vision for the future—what does success look like? What are your goals?

_____

_____

_____

_____

4. Who are some prospective candidates who might share your vision for the future and be eager to learn the key skills required for success, if they don't already possess them?

_____

_____

_____

_____

5. Identify one candidate, and use the following framework to organize your outreach to them.

WHO Who is the request for?	WHAT What is it you want them to do?	HOW What is expected; how do you want them to engage?	WHY Why did you pick them?
	Participate in a DEI succession plan		
FULLY ASSEMBLED REQUEST			

6. How might you help this candidate, and candidates in general, gain the skills and experience needed to succeed in this leadership role?

_____

_____

_____

_____

UNDERSTAND YOURSELF

EXPAND YOUR CAPACITY

RELY ON OTHERS

FIND YOUR PLACE

DIAGNOSE INEQUITY

CHAMPION INCLUSION

ADDRESS CONFLICT AND HARM

ORGANIZE A MOVEMENT

REIMAGINE SYSTEMS

ACHIEVE DEI

7. When and how will you be ready to pass leadership responsibilities on to those who come after you? What work do you have to complete before you feel ready? What roles might you continue to play after you pass the torch?

REFLECTION QUESTIONS

1. If there was one thing you were particularly excited for those who come after you to do, what might that be?

---

2. How did you gain the skills required to do DEI work effectively? How might you make that experience easier or more straightforward for your successors?

---

3. What was it like brainstorming prospective successors to you and your work? If you had trouble thinking of people, how might you cultivate those relationships before revisiting this exercise?

---

4. As you continue on your DEI journey to achieve the outcomes you envision, what role might succession planning play in your future?

_____

_____

_____

_____

NOTE

53. NIH: Office of Human Resources. "Succession Planning: A Step-by-Step Guide." NIH: Office of Human Resources, March 24, 2021. https://hr.nih.gov/sites/default/files/public/documents/2021-03/Succession_Planning_Step_by_Step_Guide.pdf.

UNDERSTAND YOURSELF

EXPAND YOUR CAPACITY

RELY ON OTHERS

FIND YOUR PLACE

DIAGNOSE INEQUITY

CHAMPION INCLUSION

ADDRESS CONFLICT AND HARM

ORGANIZE A MOVEMENT

REIMAGINE SYSTEMS

ACHIEVE DEI

40

Sustain Yourself

Breathe.

In for four counts, and out for six.

Now, one more time.

Breathe.

We cannot sustain each other unless we sustain ourselves; we cannot sustain ourselves unless we sustain each other. Each of the last 39 exercises was a challenge to yourself to build up your own capacity and capability to achieve diversity, equity, and inclusion no matter your role, no matter your organization, no matter your power or privilege or access or resources, to work alongside and with others in the long journey to better organizations and a better world.

This last exercise is a challenge as well, but in a different way. It's a challenge for you to reach deep down and embrace what it takes to sustain yourself. To give yourself permission to feel and actualize things that may not have come easily to you before, if ever: rest, comfort, joy, love, hope, and more. Of course, the work matters. *And*, it can be easy to lose ourselves in it and forget that at the end of the day, *we* matter too, in ways that have nothing to do with what we're able to do or what we're able to achieve.

Sustaining ourselves requires that, more than anything, we recognize that our inherent worth is more than what we produce or achieve or do, and take steps to nourish, celebrate, and protect that worth—situating our final exercise where the very first began.

> **PRACTITIONER'S TIP**
>
> Build purpose outside of work. Yes, even if work itself is DEI, and even if it's already immensely purposeful! If all the meaning in our lives exists in the work we do every day, we can wrap our sense of self and identity up unhealthily in it. Work failures become personal failures. Work relationships become our only relationships. Even if you find meaning, purpose, and even sustenance through work, make a strong effort to find these same things in at least one other place as well. Doing so can give you valuable perspective on your relationship to work and can offer an outlet when you most need it. Use this exercise to reconnect with your most aspirational self.

LEARNING GOALS

- Identify activities that nourish our inherent worth.
- Actualize rest, comfort, joy, love, and hope.

UNDERSTAND YOURSELF

EXPAND YOUR CAPACITY

RELY ON OTHERS

FIND YOUR PLACE

DIAGNOSE INEQUITY

CHAMPION INCLUSION

ADDRESS CONFLICT AND HARM

ORGANIZE A MOVEMENT

REIMAGINE SYSTEMS

ACHIEVE DEI

INSTRUCTIONS

Answer the exercise questions to brainstorm how you might validate your self-worth and actualize rest, comfort, joy, love, and hope in your own life.

1. What do you love—or what are you proud of—about yourself? There are no wrong answers to this question. You can share things about your body, your personality, your values, or anything else.

_____

_____

_____

_____

2. What are some relationships that are most important to you? Why are they meaningful?

_____

_____

_____

_____

The next questions will ask you about times in your life you experienced certain emotions or feelings and will challenge you to reconnect with them. Push yourself; be creative in your answers!

3. When was the last time you felt truly _rested_? What did it feel like?

_____

_____

_____

_____

4. What might you do to be able to feel that way again today, this week, or this month?

_____

_____

_____

_____

5. When was the last time you felt a sense of genuine *comfort*? What did it feel like?

_____

_____

_____

_____

6. What might you do to be able to feel that way again today, this week, or this month?

_____

_____

_____

_____

7. When was the last time you felt a sense of pure *joy*? What did it feel like?

_____

_____

_____

_____

8. What might you do to be able to feel that way again today, this week, or this month?

_____

_____

_____

_____

9. When was the last time you felt like you were *loved*? What did it feel like?

_____

_____

_____

_____

UNDERSTAND YOURSELF

EXPAND YOUR CAPACITY

RELY ON OTHERS

FIND YOUR PLACE

DIAGNOSE INEQUITY

CHAMPION INCLUSION

ADDRESS CONFLICT AND HARM

ORGANIZE A MOVEMENT

REIMAGINE SYSTEMS

ACHIEVE DEI

10. What might you do to be able to feel that way again today, this week, or this month?

_____

_____

_____

_____

11. When was the last time you felt a sense of _hope_? What did it feel like?

_____

_____

_____

_____

12. What might you do to be able to feel that way again today, this week, or this month?

_____

_____

_____

_____

13. When was the last time you felt a sense of _purpose_ outside of work? What did it feel like?

_____

_____

_____

_____

14. What might you do to be able to feel that way again today, this week, or this month?

_____

_____

_____

_____

TO SUSTAIN DEI WORK,
WE NEED TO KNOW HOW TO DO IT WELL.

BUT TO SUSTAIN OURSELVES,
WE NEED TO *BE* WELL TOO.

TO ACHIEVE DEI, WE NEED TO DO ENOUGH
TO MOVE THE NEEDLE,

BUT NO MATTER HOW MUCH WE DO,

REMEMBER THAT AS YOU ARE,

YOU ARE ENOUGH.

GUIDED ROADMAPS

These curated sets of exercises can guide your reading and rereading experiences. Pick the sets that most align with your current goals for a shorter, more focused learning sprint.

INTERNAL REFLECTION

EMOTIONAL INTELLIGENCE

IDENTITY AND DIFFERENCE

INCLUSIVE LEADERSHIP

POWER AND INFLUENCE

ANALYSIS AND ASSESSMENT

MOVEMENT BUILDING

STRATEGY

KEY DEFINITIONS

Accessibility. A design philosophy that centers the needs and experiences of people with disabilities.

Allyship. A strategy to achieve any DEI outcome whereby people possessing socially advantaged identities utilize those advantaged identities to create change.

Belonging. The extent to which people feel part of a larger whole in a group setting. It's a metric by which we measure inclusion.

Bias. A tendency (intentional or not) toward certain people, groups, ideas, or outcomes. Also, *unconscious bias* refers to bias in individual thinking, and *structural bias* refers to biases in processes, policies, or practices.

Coalition. An alliance (often temporary) of different individuals, groups, or entities for joint action or to achieve a common goal.

Culture. The shared but unspoken values, assumptions, and expectations for behavior in an environment that are embodied by rituals, stories, and beliefs.

Diversity. The workplace demographic composition in an organizational body that all constituent populations trust as representative and accountable.

Employee resource groups (ERGs). Also called affinity groups. Voluntary groups of workers that form, based on a common interest or background, for shared community and resources.

Equity. The presence of success, well-being, and enablement, and the absence of discrimination and mistreatment, on all levels for constituent populations.

Inclusion. The felt and perceived environment in an organizational body that all constituent populations trust as respectful and accountable.

Institutional knowledge. The often unspoken knowledge about an organization's history, change over time, memory, insights, skills, tactics, and relationships that the longest-serving members of organizations often possess.

Intersectionality. An analytical perspective in which different dimensions of identity, difference, and inequity are considered concurrently.

Justice. The principle that people receive what they deserve through the dismantling of barriers in society and the rectifying of historical harms.

Marginalized/minoritized/disadvantaged/underserved population. A group sharing an identity, experience, or attribute that has lesser power and endures greater hardship in an environment as a result of that identity, experience, or attribute.

Microculture. Culture—defined by a shared set of expectations, assumptions, rules, and beliefs—on a small scale.

Organizational culture. The underlying beliefs, assumptions, values, expectations, and ways of thinking and doing that drive the behavior of people within an organization.

Performative. A critique of an action as ineffective or insincere, often due to its superficiality or lack of substance or the lack of trust the critiquer has in the actor.

Positionality. How one's unique combination of identities and power affects their experiences in an environment.

Power. The ability to decide, define, influence, or change outcomes of any kind on individual, interpersonal, or organizational levels.

Privileged/majoritized/advantaged/overserved population. A group sharing an identity, experience, or attribute that has greater power and endures lesser hardship in an environment as a result of that identity, experience, or attribute.

Psychological safety. The individual, team, or organization-level belief that a given environment is safe for interpersonal risk taking, vulnerability, and failure.[54]

Subtle acts of exclusion (SAE). Also called microaggressions. Statements, actions, or incidents regarded as instances of indirect, subtle, or unintentional discrimination against members of a marginalized group.[55]

---

54. Leading Effectively Staff. "What Is Psychological Safety at Work? How Leaders Can Build Psychologically Safe Workplaces." Center for Creative Leadership, May 10, 2023. https://www.ccl.org/articles/leading-effectively-articles/what-is-psychological-safety-at-work/.

55. Jana, Tiffany, and Michael Baran. *Subtle Acts of Exclusion: How to Understand, Identify, and Stop Microaggressions*. Berrett-Koehler, 2020.

ACKNOWLEDGMENTS

Thank you to the readers, leaders, and practitioners who finished *DEI Deconstructed*, reflected on the impact they wanted to make, and reached out to me hungry for more. That fire is the reason for this workbook's existence.

Thank you to the team at Berrett-Koehler once again, especially Lesley Iura and Charlotte Ashlock, for guiding me through the experience of writing a workbook—and for believing in me when I came to you with the ludicrous idea to turn what was originally going to be a modest recapitulation of the source material into a whopper of a sequel.

Thank you to my wife, Andrea, for your unwavering smile, patience, and support, especially when I was bemoaning my looming deadlines (approximately three times a day). Having you in my life is a celebration.

Thank you to Meghan, for creating a space for healing, resting, and reflecting.

Thank you to Andrea, Reena, Rich, Kristen, Danger, Melissa, Crystal, Gayle, Amy, and Emmy for all your love. I speak often about the power of having a community outside of work, and that community is all of you. I love you all. Thank you for having me.

Thank you to my LinkedIn community for reminding me that the promise of social media as an organizing force for good isn't dead just yet, for pushing me to do better, and for taking the ideas I put out into the world and turning them into incredible work.

And thank you to you, dear reader and practitioner (because by this point, that is exactly what you've become), for using your knowledge, influence, and power to create the world we all deserve. May you build on the tools I've shared here to build an incredible future.

INDEX

ABOUT THE AUTHOR

LILY ZHENG (they/them) is a no-nonsense Diversity, Equity, and Inclusion strategist, consultant, and speaker who helps organizations and leaders achieve the DEI outcomes they aspire to. Lily is a dedicated practitioner and advocate named a Forbes D&I Trailblazer, 2021 DEI Influencer, and LinkedIn Top Voice on Racial Equity and whose work has been featured in the *Harvard Business Review*, in the *New York Times*, and on NPR. They are the author of *Gender Ambiguity in the Workplace* (2017), *The Ethical Sellout* (2019), *DEI Deconstructed: Your No-Nonsense Guide to Doing the Work and Doing it Right* (2022), and most recently *Reconstructing DEI: A Practitioner's Workbook* (2024). Lily holds an MA in Sociology and BA in Psychology from Stanford University. They live with their wife in the San Francisco Bay Area and can frequently be found putting together yet another all-black outfit and enjoying good Chinese food.

NOTES

NOTES

NOTES

NOTES